Does Job Training Work?

T0383955

**Conservation of Human Resources
Studies in the New Economy**

Does Job Training Work? The Clients Speak Out, Eli Ginzberg, Terry Williams, and Anna Dutka

New York's Financial Markets: The Challenges of Globalization, edited by Thierry Noyelle

Immigrant and Native Workers: Contrasts and Competition, Thomas R. Bailey

Beyond Industrial Dualism: Market and Job Segmentation in the New Economy, Thierry J. Noyelle

Computerization and the Transformation of Employment: Government, Hospitals, and Universities, Thomas M. Stanback, Jr.

Technology and Employment: Concepts and Clarification, Eli Ginzberg, Thierry J. Noyelle, and Thomas M. Stanback, Jr.

Does Job Training Work?

The Clients Speak Out

Eli Ginzberg
Terry Williams
and Anna Dutka

with a Foreword by David Lacey

Routledge
Taylor & Francis Group

LONDON AND NEW YORK

First published 1989 by Westview Press

Published 2018 by Routledge
52 Vanderbilt Avenue, New York, NY 10017
2 Park Square, Milton Park, Abingdon, Oxon OX14 4RN

Routledge is an imprint of the Taylor & Francis Group, an informa business

Library of Congress Cataloging-in-Publication Data
Ginzberg, Eli, 1911–
  Does job training work?
  (Conservation of Human Resources studies in the
new economy)
  1. Occupational training—Pennsylvania—Philadelphia
Metropolitan Area. I. Williams, Terry M. II. Dutka,
Anna B. III. Title. IV. Series.
HD5715.4.P5G56 1989   331.25′92′0974811   88-36277

ISBN 13: 978-0-367-00346-3 (hbk)
ISBN 13: 978-0-367-15333-5 (pbk)

Contents

Foreword

When the senior author of this book, Eli Ginzberg, asked me to write a foreword, I accepted with enthusiasm and a firm sense of purpose. My conviction about the importance of this work stems from the fact that, despite more than $100 billion spent on employment and training from 1962 to 1982, no one has ever talked to the customers—potential and actual—about their views of its effectiveness and relevance to their lives.

In my first year as President and CEO of the Philadelphia Private Industry Council (PIC), I defined our customers—both trainees and employers—as critical constituents for our work. Later in this foreword, I will describe what we learned about our customers in 1985, and what we did in response to their views of publicly financed employment and training work.

The seed for this book was planted in the Spring of 1987. At that time, the Philadelphia PIC ranked number one on four of the seven performance standards mandated by the Commonwealth of Pennsylvania. We at the PIC were doing very well, but I wanted to learn more about the trainees' decisions to participate in our programs. That decision, when positive, led to effective job placements and helped each person get on a path toward self-sufficiency. When negative, another person stood outside the local employment and training system and was still dependent on the direct and indirect income from welfare. In this context, I asked Eli Ginzberg and his colleagues—Terry Williams and Anna Dutka—to construct a research design which would answer the question, Why does a person participate in a program? Also, what factors—positive or negative—influenced this decision?

This book reports the findings of a 1987 survey of our customers. Paying attention to our customers is not a new phenomenon. In fact, this interest led, in the Spring of 1985, to a survey which has had lasting effects on our operational practices. I have summarized in the following paragraphs the key findings from PIC's 1985 customer survey.

In 1985, the Philadelphia PIC defined itself as a "training-based bridge" which connects motivated, interested people with employers who want to hire productive, effective employees. As a training-based bridge, PIC has two key customers—the trainees and the employers. Both customers count, but each has its own particular needs. The PIC pays attention to our trainees' needs by developing and implementing programs and services which respond to them. Our employment and training business is set up to deliver productive, effective people to our employer-customers. Although most successful private sector businesses endeavor to be customer-sensitive, most, if not all, employment and training organizations rarely think along these lines. Even when they do, their interest is focused primarily on the trainee. At the Philadelphia PIC, we focus on both customers. We need the trainee and the employer to have a successful, well-functioning employment and training system and business. Exclusive focus on one alone does not lead to an effective delivery system.

If we need both the trainee and the employer, then we must ask, "What do our customers want from the PIC?" When we asked our trainees, they said:

- *First*, they wanted the payoff of a job. For them, that was the real test of the value of any training program. Would the training lead to a job?
- *Second*, they sought quality and dependability. They favored programs where they learned marketable skills and could depend on the training provider to work with them and assist them with their job search activities.
- *Third*, they preferred the location of the training site to be near their residence. Most Philadelphians have a strong preference for living, training, and working in the same community.
- *Fourth*, they insisted on a reduction in the number of problems confronted during the process of enrolling in a program. Also, they requested a reduction in the time between a trainee's expression of interest in a program and enrollment.

From our trainees' perspective, these four "wants" represented "make or break" factors for their participation in a PIC-sponsored program.

In a similar manner, we asked our employers the same question. Their responses were:

- *First*, they are interested in hiring productive, effective people—people who can "do a job."
- *Second*, all new hires must have sound basic skills—reading, math, and English language skills at an eighth grade level.

- *Third,* they prefer people who have good work habits and a positive attitude toward work. It is a major plus if a person can work effectively alone or as a member of a work team.
- *Fourth,* they disliked an approach to employers which over-emphasized their social responsibility. They were interested in new hires who could do a job and wanted to work with PIC on that basis.

For employers and trainees alike, it is important to ask, "What do you want?" In the asking of the question, we have learned much about our customers. This learning has caused us to refine and fine tune our operations, and to work differently. Of equal importance is PIC's response—the delivery of programs and services. Having asked the question of our customers, what did PIC intend to do about their respective and well-defined needs?

Listening to our customers has led the Philadelphia PIC to take new and different approaches to employment and training work. Some of our new initiatives—responsive to our trainees' needs—include:

1. *The PIC Referral Center (PRC) Network.* We have established the PRC network to act as our recruitment and referral agent. There are thirty-eight community-based PRCs and these earn an average of $20,000 per annum for this work. In 1987–1988 alone, the top three PRCs earned more than $40,000 each. The major advantage of the PRC network is its accessibility to the people who want to work. Every prospective trainee has a PRC located within a short distance of his home. Overall, the PRCs account for 70 percent of our enrolled trainees.
2. *Keep Philadelphia Working (KPW).* KPW is a musical revue—combining entertainment and information—used to promote PIC's summer employment program called Phil-A-Job. This revue quadrupled our enrollment rate in the high schools.
3. *One-Stop Training.* We have selected training providers capable of delivering a comprehensive employment and training program at a single site. One-Stop Training provides basic educational skills, work preparation, and occupational skills. One-Stop Training yields a higher placement rate (84 percent in 1987–1988) and a more consistent retention rate (mid-70s to low-90s) after initial employment than conventional methods.

Increasing numbers of Philadelphians have benefitted from these (and other) initiatives. In short, our trainees can count on the PIC to deliver what is needed. In fact, over the past three-and-a-half years, more than

13,400 Philadelphians have been placed in permanent jobs and their annualized earnings exceed $130 million.

PIC's approach to employers has also changed. The major changes include:

1. *A New Marketing Strategy.* PIC now markets to employers, using an effectiveness strategy rather than a guilt strategy. Employers make hiring decisions based on their assessment of a person's capacity to do a job well and completely. An employer cannot be compelled to hire, based on a social service or social responsibility emphasis. Both terms are code words for guilt. Our effectiveness marketing strategy has resulted in a 250 percent increase in the number of companies which accept PIC people. We now work with 1,500 employers, compared to 600 three-and-one-half years ago. Also, we now do a lot of "repeat" business with our employers.

2. *Employer Input for PIC Training.* In all of our training programs, we use the employer's hiring requirements as a standard for determining successful completion of the program. Also, we have established a PIC Board-appointed Program Evaluation Committee (PEC) to review all training proposals and recommend funding. The PEC is composed solely of private sector business people.

   As a final comment, we invite private sector employers to participate as special advisors on new projects, e.g., the Philadelphia Youth Service Corps. The combination of these activities ensures employers that PIC graduates are prepared for work and meet their hiring requirements.

3. *An Operational Practice of Starting Small and Growing Over Time.* In responding to a prospective employer's hiring order, we prefer to start with a small number of hires and to deliver well for the employer. We have adopted this operational practice to build a strong, sustained relationship with each employer and to achieve the requisite placement outcomes.

Customer responsiveness—to both our trainees and our employers—has ensured that PIC has an effective employment and training business which delivers. This book is further evidence of our willingness to reach out to one group of our customers—PIC trainees. We have talked to those who do participate and those not yet participating. We have learned from their comments and will put in place the necessary operating conditions to make PIC-sponsored programs more attractive. For example, career preparation, and not short-term earnings, is the dominant and overriding concern of young people participating in Phil-A-Job. In 1989, we will establish a set of educational, work, and cultural choices which will lead directly to careers. As part of the 1989 educational component, we will distribute this book and insist that the chapters on customer response be mandatory reading. Through these chapters, young people will take a critical look at their living practices and define their personal agenda and action plan for pursuing constructive choices in the future.

This work—both the book and PIC's operational practices—points to the necessity for reaching out directly and purposefully to our customers. The PIC team which was responsible for that well-conceived outreach in 1987 was Nate Causley, Patt Irving, Deborah Johnson, and John Walsh. Their strong interest and continued involvement made, and continue to make, the difference in our outreach.

The research members of the PIC team were Eli Ginzberg, senior author, and his very able collaborators—Terry Williams and Anna Dutka. This team had significant strengths that are evident throughout this book. Eli Ginzberg has written for more than five decades about manpower issues, and had a direct connection to employment and training work for almost two decades. Eli's perspective made it possible for him to extract the lessons to be learned in each chapter of trainee interviews and to write convincingly and authoritatively about the national policy implications in the concluding chapter.

Terry Williams has an incredible capacity to establish "instant rapport." His warmth and good feelings about the people he interviewed drew out very frank and strongly felt opinions. Terry moved in and out of new situations and engaged every person during his interviews. Terry's first-rate interviewing skills have made the chapters about the trainees fresh, informative, and compelling as he uses their words and dialect to tell a convincing and moving story.

Anna Dutka—a senior researcher at Columbia University's Conservation of Human Resources—stretched everyone's perspective during the study. That perspective, combined with her talent for pulling together the research and PIC teams into a well-functioning unit, placed the views of these Philadelphians into a more meaningful framework.

Working together, the PIC team and the research team led by senior author, Eli Ginzberg, have created a moving, compelling, and authoritative story about our customers' interests and needs. PIC's key customers—our trainees and our employers—are the primary reasons for, and the major beneficiaries of, this work. Based on what we have learned from both of them, PIC's strong resolve is always to keep talking to our customers. That dialogue is essential to *keep Philadelphia working.*

David Lacey

Acknowledgments

A good many individuals and organizations facilitated our research, the findings of which are reported in this book. Our primary indebtedness is to David Lacey, President and CEO of the Philadelphia PIC, who asked us to undertake the study and who facilitated our work at every stage.

His principal associates, Natalie Allen, vice-president and chief operating officer; Conni Freeman, vice-president of training; and Patricia Irving, vice-president of youth operations and program services, were highly supportive.

Special thanks are due John Walsh, manager of Neighborhood Relations and Client Services, who worked with us at every stage of the survey of the PIC referral centers, which provided the basis of our analysis of the "do not respond" problem. Andrea Powell, neighborhood relations specialist, and Amalfi Finnerty, referral center coordinator, were also helpful in this facet of our work.

Finally, we wish to thank the staffs of the PIC referral centers who made time in their busy schedules to inform us about their multiple operations and to call our attention to many strategic and operating questions. Our greatest debt is to the large number of PIC clients who were willing to let us talk with them at length and who answered our many questions straightforwardly and without sugar-coating their replies. It is their book as much, or even more, than it is ours.

Eli Ginzberg

1

The Philadelphia
Private Industry Council

In the two decades between the Manpower Development and Training Act (MDTA) of 1962 and the expiration of the Comprehensive Employment and Training Act (CETA) in 1983, the federal government spent about $100 billion on programs to provide training and jobs for the hard-to-employ. Charges of serious mismanagement of these federal funds, probably grossly exaggerated, and the perception that relatively few CETA enrollees obtained full-time jobs in the private sector led the Reagan administration to seek an end to federal support for employment and training programs. However, the severe depression of 1982, which raised the unemployment rate above the 10 percent level, forced the administration to accept a congressional compromise: the federal government would cease financing public service jobs but would continue to make training and related employability assistance available for the hard-to-employ. A major aim of the new Job Training Partnership Act (JTPA) of 1982 was the expanded role of the business community that henceforth was to be directly involved in the design and oversight of the federally funded programs.

Title I of the Act reflected the concept of the "New Federalism" under which federal block grants are made to the states with a minimum of supervision. Primary oversight responsibility for the JTPA rests with state governors, but 78 percent of the federal funds which they receive must be focused on the Service Delivery Areas (SDAs) according to the federal formula based on the distribution of poor people and the number of unemployed persons. A state's share of 22 percent is divided into four "set-asides": 8 percent for coordination of educational programs with JTPA; 6 percent for performance awards and incentives to provide more assistance for the most needy; 5 percent for state administration; and 3 percent for older workers.

The Private Industry Councils (PICs), with a predominance of business representatives and local elected officials, are jointly responsible, under congressional stipulation, for selection of program administrators and oversight of training programs.

Three additional operating principles were built into the JTPA: a results-oriented approach requiring that training culminate in both a high proportion of enrollees being placed in unsubsidized jobs and, hence, reduced welfare dependency; the prohibition of public service employment; and a limitation on support services, including training stipends, to inhibit the development of "professional trainees."

Title II of the Act, Training Services for the Disadvantaged, covers the largest part of the JTPA population. Title IIA, Adult and Youth Programs, defines participant eligibility and acceptable forms of training and services. As in previous legislation, eligibility is restricted largely to the "economically disadvantaged." Unemployment is not, however, a precondition. In addition, those with special barriers to employment, such as school dropouts, teenage parents, non-English speakers, older workers, displaced workers, substance abusers, etc., may participate even if they are not economically disadvantaged.

In addition to spelling out the eligibility criteria, Title IIA established acceptable program services and types of training. Aside from prohibiting public service employment of any kind, local autonomy in designing programs for adults and youth is encouraged. A total of twenty-eight kinds of services may be provided with JTPA funds, in addition to special youth programs (education for employment, preemployment skills training, school-to-work transition assistance programs, etc.) within stipulated time limits. Even subsidized employment in the private sector or with nonprofit organizations is permitted as a "rehearsal" for work in the case of disadvantaged youth who have never worked before and for adults who have been out of the work force for some time. Pre-enrollment screening is encouraged to facilitate a better fit between need and remediation.

Training includes classroom training (CT) in basic education, leading in some cases to a GED, occupational skills training, or a combination of the two, on-the-job training (OJT) in an actual work setting with the employer reimbursed for part of the trainee's wages, job search assistance, and work experience.

Training is restricted to occupations in demand locally or in the area to which the trainee may relocate. Among the more popular types of classroom training are office technology (word processing, computer operation) and general clerical training. Other courses range from licensed practical nurse to home health aide, to craft and operative skills, bank teller, electronic production work, etc. Course time ranges from two weeks to a maximum of two years in a community college.

OJT programs usually have a maximum duration of twenty weeks and if a worker's performance is satisfactory it is expected that a job offer will be made. According to *The Job Training Partnership Act, A Report by the National Commission for Employment Policy*, published in 1987, OJT and job search assistance resulted in the highest level of job placements in 1985.

Title IIB, Summer Youth Programs, is intended mainly for disadvantaged youth between the ages of sixteen and twenty-one but is available also to fourteen- and fifteen-year-olds. These programs offer remedial education, work experience, job search training, and OJT.

Before outlining the specifics of the Philadelphia Private Industry Council, the contours of the Philadelphia economy require a brief review.

According to a recent issue (1988) of *Employment and Earnings*, published by the U.S. Bureau of Labor Statistics, there are about 778,000 persons employed in Philadelphia, of which 147,000 are government workers and 21,000 work for railroads. Approximately two in five were employed in services, slightly less than one in five in manufacturing, and one in six in retail trade. These three industry groups together furnished 75 percent of all jobs held by Philadelphia workers. On a disaggregated basis, the health care industry was the single largest provider of jobs (12 percent), followed by finance, insurance, and real estate (11 percent), business and miscellaneous business services (10.5 percent), and education (7.6 percent).

An analysis of business establishments by the number of employees confirms the fact that Philadelphia is a city of small businesses. Over half of the firms have between one and four employees and 85 percent have fewer than twenty.

Inner-city Philadelphia is a low-wage area where many work for the minimum wage and $4 per hour will attract young entry-level workers. On the other hand, in the suburbs where jobs are expanding rapidly, $6 per hour plus some benefits has become the norm for fast-food workers and other unskilled help. This mismatch has led to exploratory efforts by the transit authority to sponsor shuttle buses between the inner and outer city; to extend city rail and bus routes into the suburbs; and to provide direct transportation services to suburban corporate parks—all with the goal of getting people to the available jobs.

Culturally, Philadelphia is a city of neighborhoods which are in effect ethnic enclaves. Many parents are fearful of having their teenagers work outside of their neighborhood or even of having them cross other neighborhoods to get to work. This parochialism compounds the severe mismatch between the areas where the jobs are expanding—the prosperous northeast—and the area of greatest need—inner-city, largely minority, northern Philadelphia.

The PIC Structure

In 1985 the City Office of Employment and Training was integrated into the Philadelphia Private Industry Council which became the key agency responsible for the publicly financed employment and training effort in Philadelphia. As a public/private corporation, the board of directors of the PIC is composed of representatives from business (who make up the majority), government, community organizations, labor, and education.

Community outreach is effected through a network of community and neighborhood-based organizations known as PIC Referral Centers (PRCs). Counting two satellite centers as independent entities, there were thirty-eight PRCs in operation in mid-1988. These centers are concentrated in northern, western, and northwestern Philadelphia, the targeted areas of need.

Many of the PRCs antedate the JTPA and several of them receive funds from sources other than the JTPA. Since PIC recognized that established, multi-funded PRCs have a better track record than newly established centers solely dependent on JTPA funds, some of which are struggling to survive, would-be PRCs must demonstrate the presence of other sources of funding for inclusion in the PIC network.

The employment and training process begins by providing information to potential clients about the role and function of the PRC. While informal information networks exist (former clients, community leaders, the church), the PIC uses the media to get the information out into the community. Some of the more sophisticated PRCs do their own advertising as well in the belief that they know better how to reach their potential clients.

The PRC serves as the initial intake center for applicants who may telephone for an appointment or simply walk in off the street. Usually interviews are not conducted immediately. Rather, applicants are given a specific date and time to return for an interview and are asked to bring certain basic documentation along with them. Only information concerning name, address, telephone number, and social security number is taken at the first contact, with the contact person adding gender and race.

When the applicant returns for the interview, initial screening and assessment take place. Educational and job history are major areas of interest as well as the existence of special problems such as welfare dependency, need for child care, lack of basic education, and limited use of English.

Screening and assessment to determine JTPA eligibility are followed by the development of an Employability Development Plan (EDP), matching the applicant's qualifications with PIC job specifications or training program requirements. On the basis of Training Program Notices and OJT information furnished by the PIC on a regular basis, the PRCs refer suitable candidates to the PIC for placement in a training slot or send the applicant with suitable skills directly to an employer with a job opening.

The PRCs are compensated for each accepted referral at the rate of $150 each for the first thirty referrals and $250 each thereafter. In addition, when the thirty-first referral is accepted, the PRC receives $1,000 to fund additional outreach and recruitment. An accepted referral is defined as enrollment in a training program, in an OJT slot, or in a direct hire situation for a minimum of at least five days.

A representative of each PRC is required to attend regular monthly meetings at the PIC where, among other matters, a monthly performance summary is distributed to each attendee. The monthly summary analyzes the performance of individual PRCs as measured by the number of total referrals to PIC, the number of *accepted* referrals, the percentage of DNRs (do not respond), the accepted referral rate (net of DNRs), and compares each to the general average for the thirty-eight PRCs taken together. The total accepted referrals determines the overall ranking of each PRC. PIC attempts to be constructive in its comments, which range from the best to the lowest:

> The PIC is extremely pleased with our relationship with _____ as a PIC Referral Center. _____'s high degree of professionalism and her exceptional skill in matching clients with training programs and jobs have contributed greatly to the success of PIC.

> It would benefit both _____ and the PIC if steps can be taken to improve the numbers listed above. We'd like to set up a meeting to discuss your recruitment.

> Extremely low accepted referral percentage indicates that more effective screening is needed. Please look closely at the high percentage of your clients being referred to jobs. Your accepted referral numbers could increase significantly if a higher percentage of your clients were referred to training programs as opposed to jobs.

Erratic attendance at the monthly meetings is also noted and for the first time in 1988 was reported to the PRCs.

For attendance at training programs, PIC pays trainees a stipend of $7 per day, $35 per week. The trainers are paid $500 per trainee when 75 percent of the group has been placed.

Interviews were conducted with the director and staff members of some of the PRCs. The following represents a composite of discussions held with some of the top-ranking PRCs as to their operating principles and results.

> *Director:* I think we have a great staff—our direct services people have a balance of compassion and toughness to them. We tell our clients to do it right or don't do it at all. We expect them to have accountability—show up for a job interview wearing sneakers and we send you home. Same if a client shows up high.

> *Vocational Counselor:* When we give a time to show up for an interview, we mean it. A young woman came in a day after her appointment—told us she had to go somewhere with her boyfriend. We told her—you get a job, you got to show up on time or you're fired. Same here—we made her go back through the cycle to get another appointment. Incidentally, I never give them an interview immediately—they have to come back. If they don't, I give them a second chance, but that's it. No keeping after them to come in.

> *Job Developer:* You got to be tough—the wrong kind of compassion gets you in trouble. People come in off the street and are not properly dressed, no work background, not job ready and if they get sent out on a job, you set them up for failure. You get the PIC angry at you because you're really wasting a lot of time and energy. Other agencies do it, but we're more realistic—maybe because we have more business people here, not just social-work backgrounds. We don't send out as many people as other PRCs, but the numbers that get accepted are much higher.

In the case of clients who have no saleable skills or have never worked, some PRCs conduct a two-week "world of work" program focused on how to fill out a job application, how to dress, how to answer questions, and how to develop "life skills" (getting up on time, reacting to criticism, etc.). The program may also include considerable coaching on how to handle the training or job interview as well as "dress rehearsals."

Those with child care, pregnancy, drug, psychological, and/or language problems are often referred to other agencies for help. An Hispanic counselor had this to say: "Spanish people, we cannot do much with them. They don't want to come to the two-week training because they have nothing to put on the resume. All we can do is refer them to ESL [English as a Second Language] classes and hope they'll come back." Non-Hispanics also have problems: "They're afraid to ask questions because it'll show they're dumb—and they're embarrassed about being on welfare and having no work experience to show on their resumes."

Not all PRCs have job developers, but in the case of those that do, the PIC has entered into an arrangement known as the "exclusivity principle" which can be of mutual benefit to both the PRC and the PIC. If a PRC notifies the OJT division of the PIC about job slots discovered through its own network, it will be given exclusive rights to those slots (unless the number of slots exceeds the capacity of the PRC to fill them) and will be paid by the PIC which in turn will receive credit for the placements.

Follow-up on job placements is left to the PIC which is mandated to follow up for thirty days before the PRCs can be reimbursed. In the case of non-PIC jobs found by the PRC's job developer, some PRCs also track for thirty days. Beyond that, tracking is variable and usually informal. An applicant may be fired and return to the PRC for additional help and a staff member may call the employer to get information on the reasons for dismissal. Shortage of staff is the usual reason given for lack of follow-up: "You're busy taking in new people all the time— you don't have the time to follow up on all the old people because you have just so many new ones coming through."

The variability in the size and quality of the PRC staff is in fact a major operating problem. Staff turnover is high and there is no uniformity in salary levels. While the PIC gives a $1,000 bonus to the PRC for successful client placement, the decision to pass on any of this money to staff workers is made by the individual PRC. Computerization of record-keeping is still rudimentary in most of the PRCs. Inadequate files result in inordinate demands on staff time.

The Training Structure

There are about fifty training programs offered by eighty-seven providers with some contractors offering multiple programs. The range of programs include: clerical (including computer operation and word processing skills), entry-level health, security, janitorial, warehousing, food services, welding, and copier repair.

As noted earlier, there is basic classroom training, occupational skills training, a mixture of the two, and OJT, which mainly attracts males. Excluding the summer youth program, the total number in classroom training and OJT totals about 12,000 annually.

The same principle of performance-based contracting which governs the compensation of the PRCs determines the compensation of the training providers, whether in the classroom or on-the-job. The PIC Business Development Representatives (BDRs), in negotiating contracts with classroom trainers, base the compensation on the *entered employment rate*, i.e., the percentage of participants who are placed in employment relative to all who began the training, not just those who completed the program. The minimum for adults is 70 percent and for older workers, 50 percent. Job placement consists of full-time (at least thirty hours for adults, twenty hours for older workers, and fifteen hours for in-school youth), non-subsidized, training-related jobs which last at least thirty days. If these conditions are not met, payment will be adjusted accordingly.

Brief reference should be made here to the issue of discrimination in the job market, which is dealt with at some length in Chapter 6. The key considerations follow: Only the banks among the large employers use PIC as an important source of new hires. Many JTPA clients with felony convictions are shunned by prospective employers. Defense contractors resort to drug testing which many of the clients fail to pass. And there is the ever-present competition from the off-the-record economy which, at some risk, will provide a marginal person considerable income for relatively few hours of work.

Special Programs

Work-Study Arrangements

Even with tightening job markets, employers require a higher level of literacy than most PIC clients possess. However, Philadelphia's "Theme" high schools—called the Academies Program—specializing in electronics, health, business, etc., have attracted students, held their interest, and kept them in school until they graduate with acceptable skills. These schools have proved successful, in part, because the curricula are up to date and the Academies staff includes job development specialists who work closely with employers and provide teachers with information about current hiring requirements in the local labor market.

A more recent program is the "Education for Employment" initiative which has been consolidated with the existing "Cities in Schools" program. The students contract to receive job training in school in return for assistance in getting jobs when they graduate. Employment centers have been opened in these schools to increase retention rates through part-time jobs.

Phil-A-Job Summer Job Program for Youth

The youth employment strategy involves linking year-round youth programs with the youth summer job program known as Phil-A-Job. Remedial classes intended for fourteen- and fifteen-year olds are available for the sixteen- and seventeen-year olds as well if initial assessment indicates a need for remediation.

Phil-A-Job represents a consortium of area foundations, the Philadelphia Urban Coalition, the Pennsylvania Job Service, and the PIC which acts as coordinator for all summer youth programs as well as administrator of the federally funded portion.

In spite of excessive paperwork and other administrative hurdles, over 24,000 young people were placed in public and private sector jobs provided by more than 1,500 employers in 1987.

Philadelphia Youth Service Corps (PYSC)

The purpose of the Youth Service Corps, modeled in many ways after the Job Corps and Outward Bound, is to provide out-of-school, unemployed youth between the ages of eighteen and twenty-two the opportunity to acquire skills and experience through a combination of hard work and education which can lead to further schooling or a job.

This is a year-round, nonresidential program which begins with a "hard corps challenge," a team-based, physically rigorous experience followed by work designed to benefit the community. The work week is 35 hours with two hours of individualized, open-entry, open-exit education. Initial compensation is at the minimum wage, followed by merit increases and either cash bonuses or education vouchers. The maximum stay is one year with six months considered minimum. Upon completion, it is anticipated that corps members will either continue their education or be placed in jobs at more than the usual entry level wage. Candidates are referred by the PRCs and interviewed and screened by the staff of the PYSC.

Single Point of Contact (SPOC) Program

This statewide program derives from the Joint Welfare Initiative and is intended to increase the employability of welfare recipients with multiple barriers to employment. These include: AFDC mothers who have been receiving benefits for more than two years or have children under the age of six, homeless individuals, ex-offenders, completers of substance abuse programs, Vietnam-era disabled veterans, persons with limited ability to speak English, and those with less than a sixth grade level of education.

Individuals are referred to training programs by the Pennsylvania County Assistance Office (PCAO) with funding to the PIC to administer the program. Instead of having welfare recipients use the PRCs as their point of entry into the training and employment system, there is direct referral to training providers for classroom training, including literacy training, work experience, and OJT. Support services, including personal and occupational counseling, job readiness training and whatever else is required to ensure retention, will also be provided.

This program, while advantageous to many of the most disadvantaged, may lead to a decline in the number of weaker PRCs because clients will bypass them to be served directly by the PIC.

2

Profiles of Youth

One of the PIC client groups interviewed for insight into how they perceived and reacted to various training and employment opportunities were youths, defined as young people between the ages of fourteen and twenty-one, whether in school, out of school, employed or unemployed, or teen-age mothers. Most of the interviewees were black, a minority were white, Hispanic, or Asian.

Interviewees fell into two groups: those between the ages of fourteen and eighteen, the vast majority of whom were still in school, and those between nineteen and twenty-one, most of whom had dropped out of or completed high school and were currently not pursuing further education although many planned to do so later on.

Unless otherwise identified, all of the interviewees were young black men or women and the interviews are presented as they were transcribed with only an occasional word change to facilitate communication.

We also had the opportunity to talk with a number of the instructors and supervisors who were directly involved in providing employment and training services to these young people and we have made use of their observations in our evaluations that close this and the two following chapters.

Saul, 14

Work

"I found out about the job from my mother. I been working here for four years. I started when I was ten years old. I teach movement and dance to five- to twelve-year-old boys and girls. I know when I first started, the first thing I had to do was learn how to take criticism. I had to learn how to be nice to people. But people here taught me what to expect. I took classes. I had been doing this for two years so I had some idea of how to do things.

"The problem [is] mostly with the money. The money is kinda low but it's better than nothing. I buy my clothes and sneakers with my money."

Family and Friends

"My aunt and uncles helped me a lot. I also went to Marcus Garvey School for positive education and that gave me a good sense of myself as a person and my history. That was very good for me. Most of my friends want me to do good things so I don't have no problem with that. All my friends say 'go for it.' The only friends I have who have gone through the Phil-A-Job program really liked it and will do it again."

Future

"I plan to get some higher education and I will go on to college for that."

Walter, 15

Work

"I found out about the program from my sister. My mother would take care of me but I decided this summer I was gonna go out and do something. My moms say if I want the job I should go for it. I would like to get about $4.00 an hour so I can buy more stuff but I can't right now. I buy some clothes right now with the money but I need some more clothes."

Family and Friends

"My sisters help me a lot. I got a sister twenty-three and another one sixteen and they both help me the most. Most of my friends say 'go for it' and even if they didn't I would still 'go for it.' My friends don't tell me what to do. If they told me not to get a job and I needed a job and something came up I wouldn't listen to them. Most of the friends I have tell me to do my best. And that's what I do."

Future

"I wanna be a basketball player."

Larry, 16

Work

"I thought the program would go longer than it did. I think it was too short. There should be longer hours and higher pay. We get $3.35 an hour and I want $3.75. But I'm in the eleventh grade and since I am, this job gives me good experience. I heard about it on Power 99 [radio station]. I would like to make more money if I could. But right now this is okay by me. Everybody says they want $5.00 an hour but they ain't gonna get it."

Family and Friends

"My mother and my father help me. I got this job because I needed to do something with myself. My parents were willing to help me any way they could.

"I don't have no friends who been to this program. Most of the time my friends be too busy to bother with this kind of job."

Yolanda (Latino), 16

Work

"I heard about the job from my mother. I think it has been good for me here. I learned how to work the computer here. And I don't think I would have learned anything if I didn't have a job this summer. I'm not satisfied with the money because almost all of it goes to the bus."

Family and Friends

"My moms is the one who influences me the most. She's the one I go to whenever I have a problem.

"I had a friend of mine who wasn't picked. She went down there. She didn't get picked. She tried two times and never did get picked. Her brother got picked. She filled out the application and then she turned them in, but they didn't answer back."

Henry, 16

Work

"When I got here they told me I would be doing the maintenance stuff and that's what I'm doing. But I wanted to have another summer job, but it didn't work out. I don't see this job as fun. I have to work too hard. I wouldn't mind having more money, something like $4.75 an hour maybe. I think some more hours would be good too."

Family and Friends

"I help my mother out and myself by working. I know I don't have to work, but it's better when you have your own money and do what you want with it. My friends are all working somewhere this summer. Some of them have to work and some of them don't. They don't say come and hang out with me so we can make more money. I don't have friends like that."

Future

"I would like to go into the Navy or the Air Force."

Julius, 16

Work

"This job is good because it gets me out of the house. But you got to remember I was in Phil-A-Job last year. I heard about it from my school.

"The money is fine with me. But I would like to have $4.00 an hour. But I just buy junk with it anyway. I also bought me a train pass. Some of my friends don't wanna do this kind of work. Some of them are too young to work. Some of them are too old to work. Some of them just don't wanna work at all."

Family and Friends

"I don't have no heroes. Well, my uncle is kind of a hero to me. He takes good care of his family. He takes good care of himself.

"My friends are like me. They work or they like to work and they don't be doing nothing bad out there. If any of them tell me what to do, I just walk away because they don't be telling me nothing."

Adrian, 17

Work

"I find it rewarding to work here at Freedom Theatre. I also work with students my age and that has some advantages. My job right now is working in the wardrobe department.

"I find most of the kids, especially girls who don't stay with the program, don't get what they expect. They don't expect to work hard. They think it's easy. Me, for instance, I thought I was gonna be an actress. I didn't expect to do the kind of hard work that I do. The whole orientation was a fluke, because they tell you one thing and when it comes to the job you do something else. In the orientation they only tell you about the good things.

"We get about $57.48 a week. The money is definitely too little. You can tell them that this is not enough money. The only thing I can do with that money is eat for two days, buy me a trans-pass, a pair of jeans, and a book for school. That's about all you can buy with $57.48. The other thing is that we don't get a lunch break. We get five minutes and that's not enough time to have lunch.

"I go to _____ High School and I pay my own lunch. The money is too low and many kids don't wanna stay around and work for so little money. Something about Phil-A-Job. Most of the kids know since this is a summer job anybody can get a job at Phil-A-Job. They feel that this is anybody's job and anybody's pay. So they feel they can go to another job and get better pay and they probably are right. My mother helps me. I don't have to work if I don't want to. You know, basically I get a job so I can have money and put something in reserve."

Family and Friends

"My mother definitely has had the most influence on me. I'm different than the rest of the kids and many of the people in my neighborhood. I live in a terrible neighborhood. It's terrible. But anyway, it's my mother, and my brother and my two sisters they have helped me too. They all go to college and that is a good thing for me to see.

"I'm more myself. I'm not easily influenced by my friends, only by my family. I know where to go for a job and I know you have to do what people tell you on the job if you wanna keep the job. I have met good people here at Freedom Theatre and that's been one good experience for me."

John, 18

Work

"Yes, I have a job in maintenance. No, I didn't finish high school. I expect to make a living and to pursue a career on my job. The first time I ever got paid for working was in summer maintenance. Then I got paid. I was in a youth job program and I was seventeen. Right now

I like accounting and sports. I'm good at all sports, football, basketball and baseball. I heard about Phil-A-Job through my friends. The good points about having a job is that it lets you get something on your own."

Family and Friends

"If the other adults in my life had their way they would have me doing electrical work and helping out at home.

"I have influence over my little sisters and my brother. Me and my friends like to go to the movies and parties. Mr. _____ in my community is a good leader, he runs the recreation center."

Future

"The good point about having a job is so you can make money and go places you wanna go. And if you can make a career out of your job that's good too. The bad point is that you can get laid off, or terminated. The most important thing about a job is you can get training, and the experience and the recognition. I would go anywhere close for a job.

"If I could change something, I would have finished school, and instead of having a job starting at the bottom I would start from the top.

"In three years I would like to be an accountant."

Emma, 18

Work

"No, I don't have a job right now. I expect to make $4.00 an hour. Yes, I finished high school. I want to get a job to have money on my own. Instead of depending on my moms, depending on myself. No, I was never offered the chance to make money off the streets.

"My first job experience was a summer job. I have skills in child care and taking care of children. Painting the windows and fixing windows, putting glass in the windows. And nursing.

"None of my friends ever used Phil-A-Job. I heard about Phil-A-Job through my school."

Family and Friends

"Yes, they expect me to make money to help around the house. The same things as my friend Delores says: To go to the movies and to buy stuff.

"No, I don't have any leaders in my community."

Future

"The point about having a job is that it may not be what you want. Some of the people you work with may have nasty attitudes. I like to work in a nice place. And I think going too far is a problem. If I could change anything it would be my attitude.

"In three years I would like to have a good job and a car."

Delores, 18

Work

"No, I don't have a job right now. I expect to make $6.00 an hour. Yes, I finished high school. I want to work to help my moms. To buy things you always wanted. I was first paid to babysit. I have good skills in helping people and I'm good at math. I have been involved in street hustling and you know girls are just as much into selling drugs as boys. Down here they say 'my girls' and it's the same as 'my crew' in New York. None of my friends ever used Phil-A-Job. I found out about Phil-A-Job through a counselor at school."

Family and Friends

"Yes, my family depends on me to make money. My friends and I go to the movies and shopping. We go to each other's houses."

Future

"The good points about having a job is you make money. I don't know any bad points. If I could change things, I would change nothing. In three years I would just like to have a job."

Charles, 18

Work

"No, I don't have a job right now. I expect to make $4.50 an hour. I want a stock position. Yes, I finished high school. Every teenager wanna work except if they got a lotta money banked up. Then if you got it banked up you wanna work because you're bored. No, I was never offered a chance to make money off the street. I do prep [work], you know, a cook. None of my friends ever been in Phil-A-Job. I heard about Phil-A-Job through the mail. I expect to get good benefits from a job."

Family and Friends

"Yeah, my family depends on me to make money. No, my little brother don't listen to what I say. I have no influence over them. I don't know nothing about it [leadership]. I stay by myself all the time. Sometimes the neighborhood could be a bad point about having a job. Because sometimes you might have had drama [fights] in that neighborhood. People be jealous and envious and folk don't want you to come into their neighborhood."

Future

"I like myself. Three years from now I wanna be in the service. I'm gonna take that test for the Navy."

Josette, 18

Work

"No, I don't have a job right now. I would like a job making $8.00 an hour. I expect to get a clerical job.

"Yes, I finished high school.

"I'm looking for a job to make a living. No, I was never offered the chance to make money off the streets.

"I'm good at braiding hair. None of my friends ever used Phil-A-Job. I found out about Phil-A-Job through my cousin. He works at the corps and he told me about it. I expect to gain experience and other things from a job."

Family and Friends

"Yeah, my family expects me to help make the money."

Future

"Nothing's wrong with me. I can't think of nothing I would change about my life. Three years from now I would like to be braiding hair as a side business. I would like to be working in a business for $20.00 an hour."

Krystal, 18

Work

"No, I don't have a job right now. I expect to make $8.00 an hour.

"Yes, I finished high school. I'm in a community college now, in my sophomore year. I'm looking for a job to support myself and my son.

"Yeah, I see it [drugs] everyday on my block. The opportunity to make money. But I gotta set an example for my son. If other adults in my life had their way, they would say, do your chores, and you can get paid. Go sweep the porch or something.

"I'm good at communicating.

"I got a job at a summer job program.

"I found out about Phil-A-Job through my high school counselor. I expect to gain experience from a job."

Family and Friends

"Yeah, they're not gonna take care of us the rest of our life. They expect me to make money. I have influence over my son. I want him to finish school like I did. There were times I wanted to drop out. And my mother said, ain't nothing out here. So I want to set an example for my son. Yes, I think the leadership program, the Big Sisters, is a good one, and it has helped me a lot."

Future

"The good point about having a job is you have your own money in your pocket. You look forward to going to work the next day. The worst thing about a job is people's attitude. First of all, I'd change President Reagan [laughter]. Three years from now, well hopefully, I'm in business or working in one. I can start as a secretary and maybe work my way up to be the president. Where I can work my way up."

Antoinette, 18

Work

"No, I don't have a job right now. I expect to make $9.00 an hour. I expect to get a job as a nurse's aide. Yes, I finished high school.

"Yes, I had the chance to make money off the streets.

"I'm good at cleaning up the house, and communicating with young kids. They come to me for advice.

"None of my friends have ever been in Phil-A-Job, through my school. I expect to meet interesting people through my job."

Family and Friends

"Yes, my family expects me to make money. My little sister, there's four of us, so she looks up to us. No leadership. They can't even stop them drug dealers from around my block, so I don't see no leaders there."

Future

"The good point about having a job is getting paid every week. But, the bad part is trying to get along with people, but I know you gotta do that. This semester I'd go to class every day. This semester I'll try to make that class. Three years from now I'll be a senior in college."

Vawn, 18

Work

"Yes, I'm a registered associate at _____ department store. I expect to make $3.90 an hour. Yes, I finished high school. I'm in college. I'm paying for tuition so I have to work. I don't like to sit around the house. I like to raid the refrigerator. I like to work. No, I was never offered the chance to make money off the streets.

"I was six or seven [first job experience]. I was asked to clean up the dining room.

"I'm good at lip service, communication. I plan to go into some kind of communications, preferably law, so I can work with juvenile delinquents.

"None of my friends has ever been in Phil-A-Job. I found out about Phil-A-Job because they sent me a letter. I expect to get benefits from a job. No one promised me anything."

Family and Friends

"No, I'm not encouraged in any way to work. I think I do influence a lot of people. There is a guy in my neighborhood who helps people get jobs. We need things like that."

Future

"The bad point is if a job is draining you, or if they are prejudiced and stuff. I'm just so stubborn, I would change that. Three years from now, I'll be in graduate school or law school."

Lovy, 18

Work

"Yes, I have a job. No less than $4.40 an hour. Yes, I finished high school. I want to work because I like things and I want to depend on myself. I don't want to depend on nobody.

"No, I was never offered a chance to work off the streets.

"I like to talk. None of my friends ever been to Phil-A-Job. I worked for Phil-A-Job for five years. I like the idea of getting into the real working world. No one made me any promises."

Family and Friends

"No one in my family expects me to work. I influence my son."

Future

"The good point is if you know the job and the money is there every week for you. I wouldn't have had a child. Three years I hope to be in the Air Force."

Juanita, 18

Work

"No, I don't have a job. I have done maintenance. I was earning $3.90. I expect to get $4.00. I went through twelfth grade. Yes, I plan on returning to school. No, there's no reason why I don't want to work.

"No, I never had the chance to make money off the street. When I was sixteen was my first work experience. I got a summer job. I don't know what I'm good at. I want to be a nurse.

"No, none of my friends have ever been in Phil-A-Job. I found out about Phil-A-Job through the mail. I expect to get more experience from this job. No, no one made promises they haven't kept."

Family and Friends

"My daughter depends on me to make money. My sister, she comes to me for advice. I like going out, and having fun with my friends. No, there's no one in the community that is a leader."

Future

"A good point about having a job is that it keeps you out of trouble. There are no bad points about having a job. If I had to change something about myself, it would be my attitude. Three years from now I expect to be in court as a lawyer."

Patricia, 18

Work

"No, I don't have a job. I used to work in maintenance. I got paid $3.50, but I expect to get $4.00. I'm going to the twelfth grade. Yes, I plan on returning to school, as soon as my son gets in school. No reason why I wouldn't work. No, I've never made money off the streets.

"[First job experience] I was babysitting my brothers and sisters. I don't remember how old I was. Yes, I was good with office work and babysitting.

"No, none of my friends have ever been in Phil-A-Job. I heard about Phil-A-Job through the papers. I expect to get some experience and money through this job. No, no one made any promises that they haven't kept."

Family and Friends

"My family isn't depending on me to make money. No, I don't have any influence in this world. I like talking and going out with my friends. I think of my grandfather as a leader."

Future

"Making money and keeping busy are the good points about having a job. There are no bad points about having a job. If I could change something about myself, it would be my bad smoking habit. Three years from now I see myself in college."

Cindy, 18

Work

"No, I don't have a job. I used to work in maintenance. I got paid $3.50. I'm going into the twelfth grade this year. Yes, I plan on returning to school. There's no reason why I wouldn't want to work. No, I was never offered the chance to make money off the streets.

"I babysat [first work experience], but I didn't get paid for it. I don't know what my skills are.

"Yes, some of my friends they're working for Phil-A-Job right now. I found out about Phil-A-Job in school. I expect to get more experience from a job. No, no one made any promises that they didn't keep."

Family and Friends

"No, my family isn't depending on me to get a job but my daughter is. Yes, my baby's father, I influence him. I have fun when I'm with my friends. I think of my mother as a leader."

Future

"The good points about having a job is that it keeps you off the streets. The bad points about having a job is the location of the job, the buses, and some people get nasty and smart some time. I don't know what I would change. Three years from now, I want to work in a hospital."

Trana, 18

Work

"No, I don't have a job right now. I got paid $4.00 to $5.00. I would like to get a job in maintenance. Yes, I finished high school. I'm looking for a job because I need money.

"No, I've never been offered the chance to make money off the street. I was seventeen; you mean in summer jobs or something? Well, uh, when I was young I was paid to babysit for my sister. I have talent in track.

"No, none of my friends have ever been in Phil-A-Job. I found out about Phil-A-Job because they sent me something in the mail. No, no one made promises they didn't keep."

Family and Friends

"No, my family isn't depending on me to make money. We have lots of people in my family who are leaders, that work at City Hall, and I'm in Little Sisters of Philadelphia, and that's good for me."

Future

"If I could change things right now, I would get away from my mother. Three years from now, I hope to have a good job and be on my own."

Robin, 18

Work

"No, I don't have a job right now. I expect to make $4.00 or $6.00 an hour. It doesn't matter what type of job I get. I'm still in school. I'm looking for work because I want some money and I want to work, to be independent. No, I've never been offered the chance to make money off the street.

"I was sixteen [first job experience] and I had a summer job. I had to sell things. It was clerical.

"I worked with kids and I also do hair. None of my friends has ever been in Phil-A-Job. I found out about Phil-A-Job from school. I just got the letter in the mail. It's too much hassle. When you fill out an application for one job they turn you down. Then you fill out another one. But, like when you get paid, they don't want to pay you on time, then they tell you you're going to get $5.00 an hour, then when you get your check it's only $4.00; stuff like that.

"Yes, they told us strictly that it would be $4.00 an hour, and when we get our check it was $3.75 an hour, and sometimes $3.50. And some people got straight up $3.00 an hour. It wasn't taxes they was taking out either."

Family and Friends

"Yeah, because they want me to be independent. They don't want me to depend on nobody. I want to do it because I want to do it. Yes, my younger sisters and them—you know, the younger kids around my way. They always come to me, 'like hey, Rob, you know.' I always be trying to bail 'em out.

"When I'm with my friends I go to movies, shopping, go to dinner and have a couple of drinks.

"I would consider my aunt a leader, because she has experience and a lot in her life. She will sit down and tell you this about what you wanna do. She helps young girls who are pregnant. She helps anybody."

Future

"Good points about having a job is that you have your own money. It ain't like you can go to anybody and say, can I have some money? You can go into your pocket and tap your 'mac' [money machine] and then you're gone. You don't have to depend on nobody.

"I know some bad points about having a job, because I work and go to school. And when you do that you don't get no sleep. I was working the night shift and going to school in the morning. And I was losing out on sleep. And when you go to school you can't concentrate because you're so tired. But that's the main problem. I love to work though. If you work on a job every day you don't have the same attitude as you do if you don't, so you have to learn to cope with it, and make the best out of it.

"If I could change anything, I would change my environment. The housing and the community. Period. Change it for my younger nieces and stuff.

"Three years from now I see myself running my own business. A beauty shop."

Anthony, 18

Work

"I don't have a job right now. I expect to get $5.00 to $7.00 an hour.

"Yes, I was offered a job selling cocaine, crack, dust, heroin, all of that stuff. But I don't wanna be involved with it. If I wanted to be a criminal I would be robbing [laughter]. Because robbing, it's easy. But I want to make an honest dollar and they don't even want to give me the chance to do that. They won't even give me a chance to make an honest dollar out here.

"I worked in an auto body shop. I was 8 years old and I used to clean up tools at the time. I got like $4.00 a week but it helped out, you know.

"I'm good at socializing with the females.

"None of my friends ever been in Phil-A-Job. I found out about Phil-A-Job because they sent me a letter."

Family and Friends

"Yeah, they depend on me to make money. My little brother he sees me and every time he sees me he thinks I have a pocketful of money. Right. He looks up to me. Right. I give him a quarter, he comes back up to me. Right. And he got his hand out, he say he wants a dollar. I can see how he is dependent on me to make money. If other adults in my life had their way, they would have me cleaning up.

"As far as my little brother, I have a lot of influence over him. He sees me out there making money, he wanna do the same thing. I be hustling changing tires for people, you know, and he's sticking right under me.

"I see Mrs. _____ as a leader. She is our block captain, and she helps other people too."

Future

"Good points about having a job is to get off the streets. The bad points about having a job is if I ran into somebody racist. I think that would be bad. But I would get to go to the boss on top of him, and explain what is going on. You know, I wouldn't have anything to do with it. I would just go talk to the head boss and let them handle the situation. You know we would all go in together.

"If I could change the environment I live in, I would change that. You know the ghetto. You know there is always things that pulls you back when you try and do something. You know nobody wants to see you, like, doing good. They always want to pull you back into the street. If I wasn't in the environment I could establish myself somewhere.

"Three years from now, I see myself flying my own jet."

Sandra, 19

Work

"No. I don't have a job right now. I expect to make $5.00 and up to start. I expect to get a job in an office as a secretary. Yes, I finished high school. I want to get some experience from a job.

"Yes, I was offered a chance to make money off the street.

"[First job experience] I would go to the store for money.

"[Skills] Running track in high school.

"None of my friends have ever been in Phil-A-Job. I like the feeling of working in an office environment."

Family and Friends

"I don't have any influences in this world. I don't know any leaders."

Future

"The good point about having a job is to work to support myself.

"I would try not to change the fact that I limit myself to certain things.

"Three years from now, hopefully, I will be working in some New York company as a secretary."

Renee, 19

Work

"Yes, I have a job. It depends on what they ask me to do. I would like to make $13.00 an hour. Yes, I finished high school.

"No, I was never offered a chance to make money off the street.

"I'm a good salesperson.

"None of my friends have ever been to Phil-A-Job. I was working with them when I was thirteen–fourteen and I'm here about every year. I expect to gain experience."

Family and Friends

"Well, my father is not dependent on me but he says if I do work I do have to pay and stay at home because, he says, nobody lives nowhere free.

"I influence my friends. My friends and I go out sometimes, dancing, to church, or to a gospel show. I don't know any leaders.

"The good point about having a job is you make money."

Future

"Three years from now, I would like to have a nice job with a nice house, and a nice rich husband."

Darian, 19

Work

"I don't have a job right now. I would like to get a job as a stock clerk. Yes, I finished high school. I want to work to make money. There is no reason why I don't want to work.

"I think I'm good as a stock clerk because it's easy.

"No, I've never been offered the chance to make money off the streets.

"I heard about Phil-A-Job from my neighborhood. Everybody was talking about it."

Family and Friends

"Yes. They want me to help out. If my family had their way they would have me cleaning up.

"I think I have some influence over my older sister, she is about thirty. Most of my friends, we just buy sodas and everything. We don't do much.

"There's no one really that I consider a leader."

Future

"The good points about having a job is that I can get money and buy special things for birthday presents, and can just buy things I need. The bad point is that the boss gives you too much criticism. Or you get accused of something that you didn't do.

"If I could change anything in my life it would be my type of music. I would like to be a jazz musician in three years."

John, 19

Work

"No, I don't have job right now. I expect to make about $4.00 an hour. I would like to get a clerical job. That's what I was trained for. I just dropped out of college. I went to _____ University.

"I was twelve [first job experience] and cleaning yards. I pick up things real easily. I have been able to work with computers.

"No one told me what type of job I would be getting."

Family and Friends

"I was brought up where you had to wait in line to get what you needed. As we grew older and as we got jobs, you know, after the basics—food, clothing, shelter—you were on your own. You took your money and spent it and if you didn't buy what you needed you didn't always get what you wanted. So, if I don't get a job I don't get the things I need.

"This woman in my community does help other people. She is a leader."

Future

"If I could change things, I would have gone to a trade school first, then to _____ University. I hope to be back in school in three years."

Karen, 19

Work

"No. I don't have a job right now. I expect to make $4.00 an hour for what I can do. I have had experience in the medical field so something around that would be good for me. I go to school now for word processing. I had to take sick leave for the medical thing, so I will be going back. So, I've been there about four months.

"I was twelve [first job experience] and I got a job babysitting.

"I'm a good listener. And if your conversation is okay—it depends on who you're talking to. I can cook rather well. I can cook pies and pastries and things. Babysitting is okay but you got to have patience. I like what I do in school, like taking blood pressures and giving injections and things like that. I didn't want to come right out of high school and jump right into college because I wanted a transition period.

"None of my friends ever used Phil-A-Job today."

Family and Friends

"To be totally honest, I'm a spoiled brat. I don't have to work if I don't want to but there are things I want for myself. Let's say, I want a new outfit. I don't want to have to say to Mom and Dad, 'hey, I need this or I need that.' I just want to just get up and go. I just want to depend on myself and not depend on any and everybody to help me.

"No, there's no one really that I see as a leader."

Future

"If I had the chance to change something, I wouldn't change anything."

Richard, 19

Work

"No. I don't have a job right now. I would like to negotiate my wages. Yes, I finished high school.

"I was offered a job making money off the streets, but I wasn't interested. They just getting themselves in trouble in the street. If they came here at least they be protected from the influence of the street. They can be making money, picking up a skill, and don't have to be constantly looking over their back, or worrying about the man popping up on 'em. The street ain't nothing but trouble.

"I worked in a supermarket [first job experience]. I'm good at cooking.

"None of my friends ever been in Phil-A-Job. I found out about Phil-A-Job through school."

Family and Friends

"My family doesn't really depend on me to make money. If there were other adults in my life they would have me cleaning up.

"I guess I have influence over my brothers and sisters. I have some influence, not much though.

"[Leader] She works for the housing people. But she is a person who helps get the houses fixed up, and that sort of thing."

Future

"The good point about having a job is to have my own money. I don't have any bad points about a job, except if a boss is too loud or something. But, basically, it's about all in one ear, and out the other. Just forget it.

"I wouldn't change nothing in my life now.

"Three years from now I would be doing the best that I can do, advancing in whatever I'm doing."

Bernice, 19

Work

"No, I don't have a job right now. To start off, at least $4.00. Yes, I'm still in high school. I was supposed to come out in '86, so I still have one more year. I'm looking for work because I have a son.

"I was offered a job selling reefer, making $100 a weight; the money is tempting, but to get locked up for drugs, no man. That ain't my kind of job.

"Yeah, well, we useta get paid for going to the store.

"Basketball, baseball, football, I have talent in sports.

' "All my friends younger than me are in Phil-A-Job. I found out about Phil-A-Job because they sent me a letter."

Family and Friends

"No, my family isn't depending on me to make money.

"I have influence over my son. He's four months.

"I don't do anything when I'm with my friends.

"There's no one that I think of as a leader."

Future

"The good points about having a job is when somebody tells you how good your work is.

"I don't know if I have any regrets.

"Three years from now I hope to be making some money."

Debbie, 19

Work

"I don't have a job right now. I expect to get paid $4.00 or $5.00. Yes, I'm still in school. I'm looking for work to support my daughter. She will be three in September. I wouldn't want to work unless they paying me enough money. Another reason might be if the supervisor or boss and I don't get along.

"No, I was never offered the chance to make money on the street.

"[First job experience] I was paid to babysit. I type about fifty words and file.

"None of my friends ever been in Phil-A-Job. They sent me a letter. I started and worked my way up."

Family and Friends

"My daughter and my son depends on me to make money. Nobody in my family works, so I need to work to help my mom.

"I have influence over my daughter.

"When I'm with my friends I watch T.V. all the time.

"No, there's no one that I think of as a leader."

Future

"The good point about having a job is that when you get a job you are not depending on anybody, and you're doing for yourself. The bad point is getting paid and having to give up my money. I hate giving away my money.

"I don't know what I would change.

"Three years from now I'll be in the service."

Keith, 20

Work

"No. I don't have a job right now. I expect to make $5.00 an hour.

"I did machine service last summer. I was working doing machine work. So, I want something like that now.

"The only thing messing me up now, not finishing high school. That's why I can't really fill these things [applications] out.

"Yeah, selling drugs. But, I don't want to do it.

"I don't remember [first work experience]. I'm good at model training.

"None of my friends ever used Phil-A-Job. They sent me an application through the mail, that's how I found out about them.

"I expect a job that can pay the doctor's bill and stuff."

Family and Friends

"Yeah, you know this is my last year in school. So they would rather see me working instead of locked up anyway.

"I have influence over my sister.

"[Leadership] I have no idea."

Future

"Three years from now, I see myself in the service. They mess you up in there. You gotta spend at least four years there."

Tammy, 20

Work

"I don't have a job right now. I expect to make $5.00 an hour. I would like a job dealing with checks and calculators and stuff like that. I have finished high school and I'm going to school now at the National Educational Center.

"[First work experience] I was eleven and I cleaned this lady's house. I was in South Carolina, and she paid me $30.00.

"I'm good at communication. I'm good at counseling groups. I'm good at a lot of things. My mother works at _____ University and she's taken me there and showed me a lot of things. She taught me not to jump around from this to that. I like working with people. Conversation is okay but not by yourself.

"None of my friends have ever been in Phil-A-Job. I found out about it from my counselor. But the first time I heard about Phil-A-Job I was in the eighth grade.

"I think the best way to attract people here [Phil-A-Job] is to advertise."

Family and Friends

"I would say yes my family is dependent upon me to get a job. But you know it's also up to the individual himself because we have to be independent, and we can't always be waiting on mom and dad to give you something. You will be a crutch. The money you get helps pay your insurance bills, you know. That money pay for all the little debts you have.

"There's no one in my community that I see as a leader."

Future

"Nothing in my life because I don't really regret nothing I did. I would just change my position. I would make more money and get an education. That's it. I plan to be in the service. I plan to be on my own maybe halfway through nursing school, saving my money and not staying too far off the base. I plan to be on my way."

Stephanie, 20

Work

"No, I don't have a job right now. I expect to make $4.00 an hour. Yes, I finished high school. I want to work to keep from being bored.

"No, I was never offered the chance to make money off the streets.

"I was first paid to babysit. I have skills in house painting and child care. I was trained in maintenance here though. The training was just six weeks and it was useful. But it was hard. We were painting warehouses.

"I first heard about Phil-A-Job from my friend."

Family and Friends

"Yes, my son depends on me to make money. When I'm with my friends I go shopping and things like that.

"There's no one in my community that I see as a leader.

"The good point about having a job is it takes you off the street. It keeps you out of trouble. The bad point is that some people have problems with their supervisors. The boss might want you to do too much. I think having a good boss is important."

Future

"I can't think of anything that I would change. In three years, I would like to get a job and not have to be on welfare. To save up and get an apartment or buy a house."

Pamela, 20

Work

"No. I'm not working right now. I expect to make $5.00 to $7.00 an hour. Yes, I've finished [high school]. Yes, I'm going to college.

"No one ever offered me the chance to make money off the street.

"[First work experience] I was nine. Yeah, I was paid to wash a dish, one dish [laughter]. I'm good at everything. I'll try to be good at things.

"None of my friends ever been in Phil-A-Job. I found out about Phil-A-Job through school."

Family and Friends

"No one depends on me in my family to make money except my kids. If other adults in my life had their way, they would expect nothing. I don't have to do anything I don't want to do.

"I have influence over my little sister, that's about it.

"[Leaders] No. Well, my grandmother. She helps other people too."

Future

"The good point about having a job is to get away from home. The bad points, well, the racism thing, that's petty.

"I would change the drug use, the freebase pipe. I would avoid that kind of thing. I would get more education because I could find a better job."

Betty, 20

Work

"I don't have a job right now. I expect to make $5.00. I would like to get a clerical job. I'm still in school, I want to work.

"No, I've never been offered the chance to make money off the street.

"I type fifty words a minute.

"No, none of my friends ever been in Phil-A-Job. I found out about Phil-A-Job through school. Okay, so you got to go through a lot of procedures and you're still not guaranteed no job. I know no job here is guaranteed, but it would help. You know like if I don't get no job, it's like I've been going through all of this for nothing. And it would be a waste of time to me."

Family and Friends

"Yes, I want to be independent to help out my family. All my little brothers and sisters want is money. When I'm with my friends I go to the movies and stuff like that.

"[Leader] My uncle. He's always on your side. He inspires. Tells you, you can do anything you put your mind to."

Future

"Three years from now I see myself as a successful businessperson starting my own business."

Richard, 20

Work

"Yes, I have a job right now. I expect to be paid $7.00 or $8.00 an hour. I going to keep that job I bet. But I want to make about that. I would like to get a welding job. Yes, I'm still in school. I'm looking for work to benefit myself.

"Yeah, I had one job going from store to store, trying to sell something. It's similar to hustling because you have to sell something on the street.

"I was like eight years old and we used to clean up houses [first work experience].

"Yes, working with cars.

"No, none of my friends ever been in Phil-A-Job. I found out about Phil-A-Job through my brother, he's in there now. I wanted to find out what it was all about. No hassle for me."

Family and Friends

"My family cut my funds off when I dropped out of high school. There's just really my brother [who] is only one year younger than me. When I'm with my friends I get crazy and get into trouble.

"There's no one that I think of as a leader.

"No bad points about having a job. My bosses have been cool. No problems."

Future

"Three years from now, I want to get my own apartment. I'm trying to get that now."

Monique, 21

Work

"I don't have a job. I would like to go into nursing because I like to communicate with people. If I had a job I would like to be paid $4.90 an hour. I would like to be a nurse's assistant. I have not finished high school. This is my last year. I'm looking for work to make money.

"The first time I was paid to do something I was fourteen years old. I was in the Phil-A-Job program. My sister is in Phil-A-Job."

Family and Friends

"My family depends on me to make money. If other adults in my family had their way, they would have me going back to school.

"I have influence over my little sister.

"When I'm with my friends we just go to the movies, and parties too.

"There's no one in my community that I think of as a leader.

"The good point about having a job is that you can spend money when you want to. You can buy things that you need. I think the same thing they are saying is true for me. The location of a job is important to me. I wouldn't wanna go too far out for a job."

Future

"If I had to change things, I wouldn't change nothing. In three years I would like to be a licensed nurse."

Commentary

Although conventional wisdom holds that a young minority person, with a high school diploma, is job ready and job certified, the facts we elicited from our interviews with individuals employed in the summer youth program reveal that the passage from school to work is much more complicated.

Our questions were kept to a minimum and were highly focused. We wanted to know the highlights of the young person's earlier work experience; their present situation; how much money they expected to make when they got a regular job; whether they wanted to work or were pushed by their families to do so; if they had ever been solicited to sell drugs on the streets; how they learned about Phil-A-Job; and what were their long-term career goals.

The information we elicited was often in sharp contrast to the "conventional wisdom" about minority youth. We stress these differences below.

Although the families into which they had been born and brought up were low-income, marginal, or welfare dependent, there had been relatively little pressure exerted on them from their parents to find part-time work once they became adolescents, perhaps because of the scarcity of jobs in their neighborhoods. A few of the young women reported that they had earned some money as baby-sitters, and a few of the young men told of helping out their fathers or getting some kind of job during the summer, but there was no pressure on them to work and supplement family income. Quite the reverse. Many of the young women reported as a matter of pride that even though they had completed high school and were approaching their nineteenth or twentieth birthday, they were not being pressured at home to go out and find a job.

They told us that they wanted to earn money so that they would not have to keep asking their parents when they wanted to buy something or do something especially important for themselves. They recognized that if they wanted to become independent, to get "free of their mother" as several put it, they had no option but to find a job. In the absence of having one's own money, one remains dependent.

How much money did they expect to earn initially? For the most part the answers fall in the $4.00 to $5.00 per hour range, a figure that was consonant with what most employers were currently paying. The widespread presumption that minority youth have unrealistic and excessive expectations as to what they "should" earn was not borne out by what these young people told us. One or two had expectations of earning a great deal more, between $12.00 and $15.00 an hour, but they were the exceptions.

In response to our question as to whether they saw anything negative about working, a sizable number brought up the point that one could conceivably encounter complications if one's supervisor was unfriendly, particularly if he or she were prejudiced against blacks. While they recognized that such a possibility could not be ruled out, they did not expect to encounter such a situation.

The major barrier that they saw in their job-seeking path was the distance that they might have to travel from home to work. This was of particular concern to young welfare mothers. But this was the principal negative associated with working that the respondents noted.

In answer to our specific probe as to whether they had ever been solicited to sell drugs on the street, the overwhelming answer was no. But several remembered that the opportunity was there if they wanted to pursue it and that they had kept their distance. One of the young women remarked that she had once engaged in selling drugs and the trade made use of women just as it did men and even referred to "our girls" when describing a group of sellers.

Although most of these young people kept their distance from the drug trade, they described many dysfunctional forces in their neighborhood that conspired to keep a person down. For instance, several said that if anybody started to get ahead by finding a job and earning a regular income, the peer pressure was very strong to pull them back to conform to the group's norm which was not to work and not to set oneself apart. A number of the interviewees remarked on the adverse effects that the deteriorating neighborhood in which they lived had on the attitudes and behavior of their friends and themselves.

The only area where these young people provided answers that in many instances conflicted with reality related to their career aspirations and goals. Several indicated that they looked forward to being a professional (lawyer) within a three-year time span although they had not yet enrolled in college! Another anticipated practicing as an accountant within the next two years, not aware that under the best of circumstances he would need four to five years to earn his CPA.

But we must quickly add that while some of these young people had unrealistic career expectations and had failed to take adequate account of the educational requirements that had to be met before one could enter various professions, many others had formulated realistic goals, especially the young women who looked forward to getting a clerical position, working as a nurse's aide, or obtaining a job as a saleswoman. A few gave their imagination free rein, such as seeing themselves three years out married to a rich man, living in a fancy home, and enjoying the good things of life, but they were aware that they were fantasizing about, not planning for, their future.

We were particularly interested in learning how these young people had become aware of Phil-A-Job. With the exception of the few who learned about the program from a member of the family who had earlier experience with it, the vast majority reported that they had never heard of it and knew nothing about it until they received a letter in the mail describing what it had to offer and the steps that the potential applicant had to take to enroll. The other principal channel that made them aware of the program was their school; some were told about it by their school counselor.

Learning about the program was a necessary but not a sufficient step to assure that a young person would get a summer job. There was still considerable paperwork to be completed and reviewed to assure eligibility. A particular hurdle was the presentation of evidence of an applicant's prior work experience. Many had worked "off-the-record" and were unable and/or unwilling to document this experience for fear of getting into trouble with either the welfare system or the IRS.

Moreover, the "hassle" was considerable even for those who had nothing to hide. The forms contained a considerable number of questions; the applicant had to provide additional documentation as to his/her eligibility. Many young people who had little experience and less skill in filling out applications found the process oppressive to the point that, with any encouragement from their peers, they often decided in midstream to drop the whole idea. Minority youth who had previously failed to negotiate mainstream institutions tended to protect what little self-esteem they retained and, rather than risk being rebuffed at the end, failed to complete their application.

What are the major "lessons" that can be extracted from this telescoped account of the young men and young women who participated in Phil-A-Job in the summer of 1987?

- Most of them revealed little pathology in their background and development: They had not had serious encounters with the police; they had not been involved in drugs; they had graduated or were on their way to graduating from high school; the principal aberration was the considerable number of young women who had babies out-of-wedlock during their adolescence.
- Despite their limited work skills, their lack of experience in negotiating the local labor market, the persistence of racial discrim-

ination that made it difficult for minority youth to be employed until the pool of white job seekers had been exhausted, and the lack of family and friends' support that could alert them to job openings, there is little or no evidence that these young people had any blocks about working regularly. Their expectations about employers' demands were on target and they had realistic ideas about the type of work that they might do and the money they could expect to earn.

The following are some of the highlights that we elicited in conversations with the staff at four different sites:

"Most of the kids don't stay in the program because they can't deal with the discipline or the bosses. Many of them have discipline problems. Many come in here and leave the next day because they don't care one way or the other. Many have just abandoned the jobs.

"Many of these kids have tremendous personal problems. We had one kid come in here and she said she would be a week late for the job because the mother was sick. I finally asked her after she got here one day what was the matter with her mother and she said her mother 'OD'ed.' You know, took an overdose of drugs. Just like that, she didn't blink an eye. Some of these kids have big problems. In past years we have had kids stealing from the snack bar or break dancing in the bathrooms, but thank god not this year."

The instructor of the fourteen-year-old group was asked about the training program and his understanding of why kids do not remain in the program. "We really have the kids for two weeks. You got to remember that the whole program is only six weeks. As you can see I teach the kids math. We not only teach them basic skills, we take them out to the workplace, to the work environment. We do field trips. We went to the *Philadelphia Inquirer*, the Police Department, and to Conrail, this time.

"Basically, we look at the kids and how they approach their own lives. You know, we try to get at what they expect from themselves. I think a lot of what is done is a backwards approach to the whole job thing for kids. I mean instead of asking kids what they want to do, we ask the employers what they are looking for. We need to provide a profile of what the job entails, then try to fit the kid into the job.

"I think we should have the kids for more weeks and a longer time during the day. It would be a lot less hectic for them and I think it would accomplish a lot more for the employers.

"Most of the kids drop out of the PIC program because of the gang influence. I also think the peer pressure and the family have a lot to do with it too. If the families don't encourage them then they are not going to do anything. I must say most of these kids come from good families.

"We have sixteen teenagers who make up our program. They are Laotian, Korean, Vietnamese. We had eighteen kids but two dropped out because of family problems. We teach the kids English, typing, job hunting skills, basic computer application, career guidance and counseling, academic and vocational skills, English as a second language, and community service. As far as the community service is concerned we have clean street efforts and a summer lunch program that feeds 90 kids every day.

"Our work study program is a well-structured one where we have supervised work study scheduled from 1:00 P.M. to 5:00 P.M., Monday to Friday. We think this six-week time frame will be enough time to familiarize our youth with the world of work and at the same time provide them with the opportunity to acquire meaningful work skills and experience to be competitive. We train the youths according to their individual background, capabilities, experience, education, and interests.

"We are also interested in encouraging racial harmony. I want to have some of the black kids from the area to work as peer counselors, teaching our kids English and our kids can teach a black kid something that they are good at, like math or computers. I'm convinced peer learning is the best approach.

"I've been working here for a few weeks as a summer replacement counselor, and I've seen many of the things that go wrong with the process. I think a lot of these kids don't know much about looking for work or when they do look they go into the office or the place with their hats on, holding their nuts, slouching in the chairs. You know. But the girls are much more organized. They are organized, I believe, because of the way they have been brought up.

"The girls have been given more responsibility earlier than boys. I noticed in my open talk with the kids that the earliest job the boys were paid for was running errands. With the girls it was babysitting, etc. This carries more responsibility than just running to the store. It is a minor issue here, but a relevant one.

"The boys would rather hit the office head on and not worry about the consequences. They just say 'I'll straighten up where it matters, when I get on the job.' Not realizing that it matters here [placement] because that's the first step.

"A lot of the kids want to know what the program is; I mean how can I get the money and do whatever it is, and get over. If they find out it's not a program, then they go through what I call the so-much-hassle phase. That is, they will go through so much hassle and after that they reach the final point [where] they just say it's too much. I won't do it.

"Then there is the proverbial 10 percent who don't want to do anything anyway. Their tolerance threshold is very low. They will say 'fuck it' at the drop of a hat.

"I think it's the perception the kids have. That has a lot to do with it. I've found that I have to almost say I have no friends in my neighborhood, because they impact so heavily in the negative on me. It's as if they don't want you to go forward, only backwards. It's sickening. I saw these two boys the other day and they asked me where I was from. I said I'm from South Philly. They said why you talk like that? I found myself saying I went to Temple and having to explain to them why I spoke the way I did. Why do I have to apologize for being well spoken? My mother taught us to speak well. I think it's disgusting to have to explain to others why I speak well. The whole idea is ridiculous. And when you don't there is always a person who says who do you think you are?

"If they want to attract more kids here they have to advertise. It takes a lot of things. People see this whole thing as a gimmick. They should take one person and let them go into the community or the school and tell people personally about the jobs.

"I was talking to some of the monitors on the job sites and I was wondering why the kids seemed so lethargic. And I thought that not enough importance is put down to the kids. This is not just a summer job, this is important, make them feel it is important. You are not just here punching the time clock you are here doing something. And when people say this is just a summer program you got to make them feel this is important. If you want them to take the job seriously you got to take it seriously too. I hear the supervisors saying to some of the kids 'this is a summer job program, don't think you are that important.' The kids pick that up too. They think, well I'm just here for the summer and they can't really fire me or anything.

"I think a lot of kids are intimidated. Many have not even filled out an application before they come here. Rather than go in and say you're a failure or show up—you go in saying, I don't need this job anyway.

"The boys especially, they would rather take a loss than compromise whatever manhood they have left.

"This is a mass production and it is not individualized, but at some point it becomes individualized.

"Most of the individual supervisors at these sites don't get any training to deal with these people who need training—people who may be hostile toward the work environment. They are inexperienced. So they don't really know. They expect them to come in and do all these things that they don't know how to do."

*   *   *

The overriding finding that can be extracted from the interviews of the youth and their instructors is that the transition from school to work, from adolescence to adulthood, is a process beset by obstacles and barriers for most minority youth, even those who have acquired a high school diploma and are desirous of getting a job and starting on a career. Their families are usually unable to assist them and while Phil-A-Job, whose purpose is short-term, offered them useful orientation, the opportunity to explore the world of work, obtain some job seeking skills, and modest training—as well as some income—the program was too short to compensate for the multiple handicaps that confronted most of these youths. They needed a stronger helping hand to make a successful transition into the world of work and adulthood, one provided perhaps by an alliance of parents, teachers and clergy together with efforts such as Phil-A-Job.

3

Profiles of Young Mothers

This chapter presents interviews with poor mothers on welfare ranging in age from nineteen to twenty-eight; one, Kim, is white and the others are black. The thrust of the interview was to elicit responses to a limited number of questions: How did the interviewees assess the balance between being on welfare or working for a living? What kind of pressures from their family or from the social workers in the Philadelphia County Assistance Office (PCAO) were exerted on them to explore training and employment? In particular, we wanted to elicit their experiences, and those of their friends, with the availability and cost of child care and the extent to which the presence or absence of such facilities influenced their decisions with respect to a job search. We also asked the interviewees to tell us about their views concerning people on welfare and the extent to which the government should be encouraged to provide jobs and support services for those who want and need to work.

The interviews below provide a representative selection from a much larger number of interviews that we conducted.

Natalie, 28

(Q) Tell me about your experience here.

"I started the 28th of August and we went to the class training for two weeks and class for me was how to dress for an interview, how to fill out an application, and just how to feel more positive about yourself when you go out to an interview."

(Q) Did you go to any other training?

"No, I haven't found a job yet. But they do send you out on interviews. I have been on quite a few interviews."

(Q) Tell me what happened at the interviews.

"Yesterday I had one and the job was answering phones and typing business letters and a little bit of switchboard. After I introduced myself I was asked to type a letter. I typed the letter and he asked me to fill out an application and I did that. And I asked him some questions about what kind of work did they do and asked him about benefits, and if they had a dress code and that was it. He said he would be in touch by the end of the week. I found out about _____ [a PIC training provider] because a friend of mine came here and got a job and I was thinking that they would find out exactly what you knew and they would send you out on these interviews and it wasn't like that when I got here. I didn't mind about the two weeks school and everything. I didn't mind about that. I mean as far as the training was concerned. That was okay. I did the classroom work. I did that part of it. I finished that. That wasn't difficult. It was something they teach you in school. You know, if you didn't know about resumes, didn't know about cover letters and didn't know how to fill out an application or how to dress, but you see I knew all those things. But I didn't know that's what it was all about when I made the call. I didn't know until after I made the call and the appointment, that's when she explained it all to me."

(Q) What kind of pay did the employer offer you?

"They offered me about $4.00 an hour. I would take $4.00 if they offered me a job."

(Q) Do you feel people can't feel well about themselves when they don't have a job?

"It bothers me because other people look at you and think that you're lazy because you don't have a job."

(Q) Do you think the government should guarantee a job to everybody who wants to work?

"Yes. But I don't think the government should guarantee that everybody have something to live on. I don't think the government should do that."

(Q) Do you think there are some people on welfare because they can't find a job that pays enough?

"No."

(Q) Why do you think people are on welfare?

"The way I see it, they have kids more than what they should have, then they can't go out to find a job because they have so many kids. A lot of people now don't really want to watch an infant up to six months, and if you do find somebody, that's costly. It's at least $40.00 a week."

(Q) What do you do about your day care needs?

"Well, my daughter just started first grade, so she's in school all day. Before, she went to preschool but that was only from nine in the morning to 2:30 in the afternoon and that gave me time to look for a job. But if a job were to come up, then I would have to make arrangements for somebody to take her to school and to make sure she was in the house and what not."

(Q) Do you have a job? I forgot to ask you that.

"I don't have a job right now."

(Q) What are you doing to increase your prospects for a job right now? Or a career for that matter?

"I've brushed up on my typing a lot. I can do forty words but that's not counting the mistakes. But I'm working on it. I picked up my old math books and went to them again. I also have a more positive [attitude] about myself."

(Q) Did the training you had prepare you for the work you will be doing?

"No, it didn't."

(Q) What was your reaction to the training?

"I didn't know it was gonna be like that. You know, I had to do something. I just couldn't stay in the house any longer."

(Q) Why do you feel people drop out of the training?

"I think some people left the training because they didn't see the training as meaning anything to them. Let me give you an example. There were two other girls who started out in the training as I did. One was Spanish and the other one was black. Now the black one she wasn't dumb. Something you know, it's like common sense, and she tried to pretend like she didn't know and was afraid to ask questions. And the other one, she was just quiet, you know? And everything she said was just negative, too negative. I get like that myself sometimes, and they just stopped coming because they were too embarrassed because they didn't know certain things. She was embarrassed to say like on my resume I put I hadn't worked for two years and she didn't know exactly what to say or how to say the reason why she hadn't worked for two years. And she was a little bit embarrassed about it. And then she was embarrassed about being on public assistance, but that doesn't make me feel embarrassed about it because I've chose that form of income. Listen, what you gonna do? You have this child to support and you gotta do something."

(Q) How would you make this program more attractive to people, to keep people in the program?

"I think you should pay people to go through training. If you had money, that would keep people in. Because like here they have a thing. I'm not sure about this but if you stay in the program for thirty days or maybe it's if you stay on the job, they give you $25.00. I'm not sure but somewhere along the line you get this money. And also they give you money for trans-passes to get to and from here to job interviews. And that's more or less why I'm in it because I couldn't afford to get the trans-passes to come out here to go out to places for the jobs. It helps you get around to a lot of places with a trans-pass. It cost $24.00 for a month."

(Q) Do your friends or family have any influence on whether you work or not?

"Yes. My sister for instance, she's negative and is always saying, 'You don't wanna do nothing. You don't wanna work. You don't have no baby to take care of because your child is in school now and you don't wanna do nothing. And you don't wanna work.' You see my mother is deceased and my dad don't live with me and I'm not real close to any of my other relatives. And it's just my sister and me."

(Q) Did you have any choice in the kind of training you wanted?

"No. Okay, well, B_____ would get these calls from these places and they would tell her what kind of person they wanted. You know this, as far as being hired for a job there was no other type of training than this two weeks class thing."

(Q) Are there any outside day care facilities for you to take your child to?

"There are places to take my child for day care in my neighborhood. If you were on public assistance and I guess somewhere the State or

the City would pay for it as far as that program went. But other places—
I don't know. All I know is the one close to my house closed down. It
was around the corner from my house. There is a church that my
girlfriend takes her daughter to. They charge around $45.00 a week.
You know that's way out of the area from where we live. She had to
take a bus to take her child there."

*(Q) I'm going to ask a stupid question, but I want your opinion anyway.
Would you prefer to be on welfare or to have a job?*

"I would rather have a job than be on welfare. The negative thing
about being on welfare is that they want to know all your business. I
mean all the way down to where you made love when you conceived
your child. And I want to know what does that have to do with it.
They want to know off the bat where the child's father is. And to know
why you can't be with the child's father at all. And they want to know
his social security number and all of that so they can put him through
the computers so he can pay. I never told them nothing about nothing."

(Q) Have you ever worked a full-time job before?

"Yes—uh-huh—I worked after I got out of high school and I was
young and wild and didn't have no kids. I worked at a cleaning company
where we went into a building on _____ Street and we cleaned offices.
We had about two or three stores to do. Then I worked at _____,
which was a printing company, where they printed up anything, like
invitations to weddings—stuff like that. I was a secretary/receptionist.
And then I worked in the State Employment Office where I scheduled
people for typing tests and job interviews with my boss. I would schedule
them and call their homes so they could know what time to be there.
I also ran off copying material for other employees in the office. I worked
at Sears and that was the best job I ever had. I would take tapes off
the racks and put the number in the computer and reading what was
on the tape and adding information or taking it off."

*(Q) Do you think the PIC Referral Center should help with day care,
transportation cost, and counseling in personal affairs?*

"I think they should help with day care because it would help a lot
of women who are really serious about the program and really wanna
make something out of themselves. It would help. I think they should
help with counseling too, because there is a guy here and I really don't
know his status here, but all I know is he is here everyday. And I
suffered a nervous breakdown after my mother had died and a couple
of days ago I felt I might be on the verge of having another one and

he sat down and talked to me and it really helped. Now he was really understanding about it and you don't find many people like that, that knows what you're going through, other than the psychiatrist that you can't afford to pay anyway."

(Q) *What do you see your future like over the next few years?*

"In three years hopefully I'll have a decent everyday job and [be] married maybe."

Kim, 24

"I read about it in the *North East Times*. And right now I'm on [public assistance], me and my son. And I live with my parents and I've been trying to look for an apartment on my own. But nobody will rent to me because right now I only have [public assistance]. So I figured I've got to get back to work and the only thing I can do that I'm qualified to do is nurse's aide. I know it pays decent but I don't really wanna do that and have to come home and deal with him too. You know. I'd rather do something else, so that's why I'm here, to have some training."

(Q) *Are you going to go into training?*

"I'm gonna go into word processing. There is another training program somewhere on _____ Street, but it does like clerical and everything. But this has the word processing in it and computers. The one on _____ I'm sure doesn't."

(Q) *What exactly does this place do for you? Does it point you in this direction of training, or do they train you too?*

"Yeah, it makes it easier. I had gone to a school where I had to get a bank loan and I had to get a grant. And I was denied the grant and I couldn't afford to go to the school. So what else can you do? This place is free and at least it gives me some practice, some skills, some confidence."

(Q) *Have you been in any training programs before?*

"I joined this school, _____. I don't know if you are familiar with it. But like I say, you have to have a grant, a bank loan, you know. You had to have money. And I had worked a part-time job at the time and it still wasn't enough because I had to have my own place. I was in for five months in the training, but I was denied the grant. They kept saying I was gonna get it, but I never did. It was a good program, but I just couldn't afford it."

(Q) Do you think the government should guarantee a job to anybody who wants to work?

"Yeah, if the people have the right qualifications. And they are willing to work. You can't just say, here, you want a job, because a lot of people don't wanna work. I think they should try to make more jobs, yeah."

(Q) Do you think the government should make sure a family has enough money to live on?

"I think the people themselves should, but I also think the government has a lot to do with that and should help."

(Q) Do you think people are on welfare because they can't find jobs to support their families?

"Well, let me tell you why I'm on welfare. Personally, because when I had [my son] I worked. I worked from high school until I got pregnant with him. And when I had him I couldn't afford day care and everything else, it wasn't enough. But if you had the free day care or the government day care which I'm trying to look into now then I can afford to work. It would be worth it, you know what I mean."

(Q) When you say you're going into training, is that what you're doing to increase your prospects for finding a job?

"Yes, sure."

(Q) How much influence does your family have on whether you work or look for work?

"A lot, because my mother is the head of the household and has always been. My father is very sickly and she's the one. You know I've always said that the more you do for yourself the better you are, that's the way I've always resolved it. But if it was his [looking at her son] father that had his way, I wouldn't be working, I would be home with my child. If you can afford to or just make it, or whatever. But not that I shouldn't like [public assistance], but that I'm better off because at least I'm looking for a job.

"My mother has a lot of influence because she went to school to become a nurse and she's the one who makes the money. And she has the only income, and I can see her struggling."

(Q) Are there people in your household who can help take care of your child?

"No, my father is very sick, which is what I've been doing—watching him and my son. And my mother works and there is no one else. Because my two brothers who live at home with us is still in school."

(Q) Are there day care facilities in your neighborhood?

"Yeah, there are day care places, but like for full time they want somewheres around $55.00 and $75.00 a week. The lowest I found was $60.00—full time. Sometimes it's ridiculous because it's like $45.00 and that's part time. But they are really good, but I can't afford them. A girlfriend, a friend of mine, has a government-paid day care center. As far as I understand she works a job and she is the only supporter and she has two dependents, so she works full time and makes okay money. And she's been working for like eight years now. But the thing is she can't afford day care either, with all her car insurance and other bills and things like that. So she got this government day care where they have these private homes and you send your child like for an hour before school and it's around your area; that's the way I understand it. And like for the hour or two hours between their ending of school and the mother's work hours. I'm not sure if they take his age, but I'm hoping they do. Now she only pays like $15.00 or $20.00 for this full-time service. It was $20.00 for full time and only $15.00 for part time, which is excellent. You know, I could afford to pay that if I was working."

(Q) Would you rather receive welfare or get a job?

"I mean, when I was first on welfare I would just say, well I'll just get that. You know, why should I work and not have anything because of the day care and all, but now, believe me I'd rather work. You know, I love my child and it's great if you can be at home, but you don't progress. You know? You don't go anywhere. I'm still doing the same thing. I'm still at my parents' home. I just wanna move on. Hopefully my son will be in school over the next two years and I'll just have to start getting out of this then."

(Q) Have you ever worked a full-time job?

"Yeah, my first job outta high school was really lousy, because it was a factory job, full-time, and it only lasted three months because my supervisor, forget it. My second job was at a nursing home and it was full time and I really didn't think I would stay, but I did. I worked there for maybe a year and three months, something like that, which is good and that's when I wound up pregnant. I had problems because as you can see I'm real tiny and I had to quit and I quit. Then I had the baby. I worked with my brother's business. I did that while I was pregnant, it was a caring companion business as a nurse's aide. I did that off and on call. I did clerical work for them. It was always on call. I did this work even after I had him. She just helped me out when I needed the extra money. That was basically it, but I worked at _____ Hospital too. I worked there for four months and that was during my pregnancy too. I was like pushing it. By then I should have cooled it and not went back to work."

(Q) Would you like to receive help from this referral center with day care arrangements, or transportation to the job?

"Yes, I would love it, but the thing I don't want is everything handed to me. But if I had day care it would be so much easier, I could get so much more done. Like now I'm being sent to training, you know. Okay, I've got all the testing done, but now I have to go and hopefully see if this one government program will take him. And hopefully it's around my area and all of that. And if it's not what am I gonna do? I can't get a family member. I don't have anyone. And if I do get anyone else it's gonna cost maybe $50.00 a week, you know if I get a neighbor or something. The big major thing for me is the day care; the transportation to the job, hey you can find a way. I borrowed a car to get here. I know a lot of people aren't that lucky, but the bus is only a dollar and you can get here. I would rather have the biggest problem taken care of."

(Q) Do you think the referral centers should help with counseling in terms of personal affairs?

"I don't know. I wouldn't think the center would do that. But if a person walks in and needs help or has an attitude or whatever then I can see them being useful in terms of counseling."

(Q) Where do you see yourself in three years?

"I plan to be working and having my own place. I don't know, like I say, I had started school before and I was going into para-legal secretary. And I had all the business courses as it was, so it can't be that hard, right? It pays good money. I thought if I ever went back to school and I got that loan taken care of right I would probably go back into medical. Right now I'm a little more determined to make it. At first I didn't think I could be going into it, but now I'm just happy to get a job."

Mary, 19

"I'm nineteen years old and I have one child. Her name is _____ and she's four months old. I don't have a job now but I went to the Academy for a couple of nights of training. That was typing and I didn't get too much out of it. I really didn't enjoy it. This training was separate from this place. I didn't like the training because the teacher didn't put a lot of effort into trying to help us get some kind of training. She was just going with the flow. I paid $430.00 from July 3 to August 28."

(Q) Did you have any choice in the training?

"Yes, I could have chose different types of training. I don't think I type any better than I did before I took that course. Honestly, I don't think so because still after I take a test for something like a job, I get nervous and tense. And I don't do as well as I would usually do if I wasn't under pressure.

"I worked as a file clerk. I was only there for two days because of my pregnancy. The guy [boss] thought that I was pregnant, but it wouldn't have interfered with my work and I explained that to him. So I just left.

"I went on that interview and I was at home and he called me and told me to come in the next day. You know when you work in a office everybody gossips and talks to the women and everybody. So I went upstairs the next day and he had hired two girls, me and a heavy-set girl. So I went in that next morning, and he said he thought the one who was pregnant was the heavy-set one but couldn't see it. And he say, now that I know it's you, my boss will kill me if he found out I hired somebody who was pregnant. So that's how that went."

(Q) How much were you paid?

"Okay, for three months you get minimum wage and after three months you are eligible to get benefits and I forgot how much of a raise. If it was room for me to move up, I don't mind starting so low."

(Q) Does it bother you not to have a job?

"Well, I wanna work. Sometimes it bothers me, but sometimes it don't. It bothers me because I like to be doing something. I can't just sit. Well, my daughter she takes up a lot of that but I still like to have my own. So sure it bothers me a little bit. My daughter doesn't want for much. She doesn't need much and I don't need much. So right now it still doesn't bother me but I still wanna work and do my own. You know?"

(Q) Do you think the government should guarantee everybody a job who wants to work?

"I don't know. Let me tell you something about the government. I took the test last September for the government and they called me for a job this summer while I was going to school. But you know what happened? I took the test, got nervous and didn't do well."

(Q) Do you think the government should guarantee that every family have something to live on?

"Yes, but some families will get something from the government and won't do nothing with it. It's hard to say."

(Q) Do you think people are on welfare because they cannot find jobs that pay enough for them to live on?

"Well, some people are on welfare because they can't find a job that pays enough for food and take care of their bills and medical coverage. They can't find a job that will help them, supply them with all of this; so there's some people in that category, then there's some people in the opposite category."

(Q) What are you presently doing to improve your prospects for a job?

"Well, I'm constantly looking and I'm involved in a program where I go to the _____ College for five weeks doing word processing and things you're supposed to be certified in."

(Q) What influence do your friends or family have on whether you work or look for work?

"My family, well, I have a great family. My mom—no matter which way, if you trying hard to prove yourself or better yourself—my mom will stand behind you 100 percent. She help you do whatever she has to do and my father, it's like if you got to go to school and get some training, go ahead do that, because your daughter is young now and when she gets old she's gonna need your attention—so I have a lot of help."

(Q) Do you know of any friends who were in your training program but dropped out?

"No."

(Q) Do you have members of your family who will help with the day care?

"My father does help me."

(Q) Are there any outside day care facilities in your neighborhood that you can use?

"I can't put my daughter in no day care because if they mistreat my child I'll be too upset. My mom's watched her for two months while I went through that training program and she's willing to help me."

(Q) Some people would rather have welfare than a job. Would you?

"No. Not me, because I believe people get lazy and don't strive to do better and just sit there and wait for a check. And then, after they get it, they just waste it and their kids don't look no better. They don't really take care of themselves. They just feed their habits [laughter]."

(Q) Have you ever had a full-time job?

"Well yes, when I was in school I worked at the school. And when I got out of school I worked at _____ for a year from January to like June. That summer I didn't work and that September that's when I took the test for _____."

(Q) Would you like to receive counseling, transportation to your job or day care help from the PIC Referral Center?

"Counseling, yes; transportation, no, I have a car; day care help, yes."

(Q) Why did you drop out of the program?

"Well, I dropped out because I was afraid of the financial problems."

Deana

"I got involved through here because of my case worker Mr. _____ who told me I would have to do something if I was gonna receive [public assistance]. You see I'm pregnant and he gave me this number and I called. And _____ told me I should get involved in some kind of training. The training is for four weeks, she didn't tell me which particular areas it would be."

(Q) Have you ever been in any training before?

"No, I haven't. This is my first time."

(Q) What kind of money would you like to make?

"A lot. I would like to make at least the minimum wage. At this present moment I would take the minimum wage."

(Q) Do you think the government should guarantee a job to everybody who wants to work?

"I don't know."

(Q) Do you think the government should guarantee that people have enough money to live on?

"Yes, I do."

(Q) Do you think that many people are on welfare because they can't find jobs that pay enough to support their families?

"Do I think that? No. I think they are on welfare because they are lazy. Let me tell you something. I know this certain family in Georgia and they just on it because they can be on it. They can work. They just lay around everyday and paying $1.00 a month rent, and they just getting all that money. And let me tell you they have finer clothes than I have."

(Q) Would you rather be on welfare or have a job?

"I would rather have a job. Because I don't like sitting around the house not doing anything. And in a way I feel guilty. The negative side to being on welfare is when you have to tell the people all of your business and stuff like that. They wanna know how much income you're making and what's your utility bills, and if you're married or single, a lot of irritating stuff. They ask if you're getting any money from this person and things like that. I'd rather be working."

(Q) What are you doing now to improve your prospects of finding a job?

"Well, I'm getting involved in this training program."

(Q) How much influence do your family and friends have on whether you work or look for work?

"Well, my father wanted me to go to college and everything, which I am gonna do in September. And I had a job when I was in Georgia which I quit when I moved to Philadelphia. My family have a lot of influence because they think I should get a job and save money, you know. So I can have the things that I want. My friends don't say much about whether I work or don't work."

(Q) Did you have any choice in the type of training you say you will get involved in?

"Yes, there was a choice. It was another kind of women's project. I don't know what kind of training I'll be involved in here."

(Q) Do you have any ideas about that training?

"No. I'm sorry I don't."

(Q) Are there any people in your household that could help you with day care arrangements?

"Yes, and I don't have to pay them."

(Q) Are there any outside day care facilities that you know about?

"No, not that I know of."

(Q) Have you ever worked at a full-time job before?

"Yes. I was working at a hospital as a housekeeper. I worked in the housekeeping department. It only paid $3.40 an hour."

(Q) Do you think this PIC Referral Center should help in child care arrangements?

"Yes, that would be nice."

(Q) What about counseling?

"I think they should."

(Q) Where do you see yourself in three years?

"I'll be in college, if I haven't graduated yet."

Commentary

It is not easy, as we noted in our discussion of Phil-A-Job, for young minority persons, even those with a high school diploma, to make a successful transition into the world of work, more particularly into a regular job with some prospects for advancement. The difficulties that young minority women face are greatly intensified once they have an infant or a preschool child to care for.

The question may be raised why such young women should be interested in getting a job, considering the fact that they are on welfare, which provides for their basic maintenance and that of their child. The answers are many and diverse. Increasingly, the social workers on the staff of the Philadelphia County Assistance Office (PCAO) have been putting pressure on young mothers not to sit at home waiting for their welfare check but to take some action such as looking for a job, returning to school to get a GED, or entering a training program so that they can connect or reconnect themselves with the world of work and look forward to getting a job and supporting themselves and their child.

But it would be wrong to ascribe all, or even most, of the efforts that young mothers are making to reenter the labor market—for most of them have had some former experience if only in part-time jobs—to the welfare staff. Most of the young mothers whom we had the opportunity to talk with had been the prime movers in relinking themselves to the world of work.

They told us of how deeply they resented the intimate questions that they had to answer in order to satisfy their social workers who kept asking them all sorts of probing personal questions.

> The negative thing about being on welfare is that they want to know all your business. I mean all the way down to where you made love when you conceived your child. And I want to know what does that have to do with it? They want to know off the bat where the child's father is. And to know why you can't be with the child's father. And they want to know his social security number and all of that so that they can put him through the computers so he can pay. I never told them nothing about nothing.

Along these same lines, this is how another interviewee saw the welfare-work choice:

> Because I don't like sitting around the house not doing anything. And in a way I feel guilty. The negative side to being on welfare is when you have to tell the people all of your business and stuff like that. They wanna know how much income you're making and what's your utility bills, and if you're married or single, a lot of irritating stuff. They ask if you're getting any money from the person and things like that. I'd rather be working.

Whether one wanted to work or would enjoy working had to be put in context: if getting a job and being able to support one's self and one's child meant not having to put up with the recurrent indignities of such personal questions, there was a great deal to be said for working. There

is no question that many of the young mothers had reached the conclusion
that getting off welfare was the preferred way for them to go.

A second powerful motivator for getting off welfare was the realization
that came with time that sitting at home and looking after one's child,
especially once the child entered preschool or school, was not a satisfying
way to pass the weeks, months, years. "I had to do something; I just
couldn't stay in the house any longer."

One of the interviewees recognized that there are people who might
opt for remaining on welfare rather than looking for and taking a job
but "not me, because I believe people get lazy and don't strive to do
better and just sit there and wait for a check. And then, after they get
it, they just waste it and their kids don't look no better. They really
don't take care of themselves. They just feed their habits."

Another interviewee reported:

> When I was first on welfare, I would just say, well I'll just get that. You
> know, why should I work and not have anything because of the day care
> and all, but now, believe me, I'd rather work. You know, I love my child
> and it's great if you can be at home, but you don't progress. You know?
> You don't go anywhere. I'm still doing the same thing. I'm still at my
> parents' home. I just wanna move on. Hopefully my son will be in school
> over the next two years and I'll just have to start getting out of this then.

Several of the interviewees reported that they very much want to get
free of their mothers, but they recognized that their only prospect of
doing so would be if they could get a job and earn an income. There
is little or no prospect for a woman on welfare to get an apartment.

We know that not only did some of the young women look forward
to the time when they could escape from their mothers, or their parents,
and set up their own independent households but that in turn some of
the parents applied pressure on their offspring to get going and take
control of their own lives.

In short, the findings from this admittedly limited sample suggest
that the presumption that welfare is the preferred, not to suggest an
ideal, state for many young mothers is a misconception. In addition to
their own motivation to assume active responsibility for themselves and
their child, most of the young women were also under varying degrees
of pressure from the staff of the PCAO or from their parent or parents,
frequently from both sources.

The fact that a great many young mothers on welfare sooner or later
came to recognize that they and their child would be better off if they
got a full-time job and began to support themselves did not mean, of
course, that their getting off welfare was easy. While most of the young

women had some prior experience in the job market in full- or at least part-time jobs, few had acquired any marketable skills or a work record that would impress a new employer. For the most part, they had held one or more unskilled jobs—in retailing, as a baby-sitter, as a telephone operator, as a general utility person in an office.

As the years lengthened between the time that they had completed high school and the time that they decided to get off welfare and look for a job, they found that their educational skills had regressed. They were less able to do fractions or other arithmetical exercises. Several told us that they had recently begun to work through their high school texts in an effort to brush up.

Aside from all of the usual difficulties that faced minority youth and young adults as they sought to get a job that would enable them to support themselves, the young mothers confronted two additional hurdles, one that they talked about at length, the other that they tended to slight in assessing the problems that they faced in moving from welfare to work. To take the second first: the fact that while they remained on welfare they—and even more importantly, their children—were each assured access to health care as a result of their being on Medicaid. Once they got a regular job they faced the prospect of losing, sooner or later, their Medicaid eligibility.

It is possible, even likely, that this did not appear to most of the young women whom we interviewed to be a major threat because many appreciated that most medium-sized and larger employers, especially of white-collar workers, offered health care coverage as a benefit after a reasonably short probationary period. In any case, the loss of Medicaid benefits was not alluded to by most of our interviewees as a barrier to their leaving welfare.

On the other hand, we heard a great deal about the problems of child care, particularly as it related to the early stages of the process of their moving from welfare to a job, especially when they had to enter training to acquire a "saleable" skill. Many believed, perhaps mistakenly, that once they were regularly employed in a job that paid something more than the minimum, circa $5.00 an hour, they would be able to cope with the costs of child care. But they were distressed and over-whelmed by the way in which the high cost of child care blocked them from taking the initial steps to move off welfare. Here is the way they saw their dilemma.

"A lot of people now don't really want to watch an infant up to six months and if you do find somebody, that's costly. It's at least $40.00 a week." "There are places to take my child for day care in my neighborhood. If you were on public assistance I guess somewhere the state or the city would pay for it as far as that program went." (But our inquiries disclosed that the state and the city together were meeting only a very small part of the total need for day care of welfare and other low-income clients.) "My girl friend takes her daughter to a center operated by a church which costs I believe $45.00 a week and that's way out of the areas where we live so she has to take a bus to take her child there."

In a relatively few instances alternative family arrangements are possible and the young mother looking for work can avoid the hassle of day care. "I can't put my daughter in no day care because if they mistreat my child I'll be too upset. My mom's watched her for two months while I went through that training program and she's willing to help me." In answer to the question as to whether there were day care facilities in her neighborhood, one interviewee offered the following elaborate insight into the situation.

> Yeah, there are day care places but like for full time they want somewheres around $55.00 to $70.00 a week. The lowest I found was $60.00—full time. Sometimes it's ridiculous because it's like $45.00 and that's part time. But they are really good, but I can't afford them. A girl friend, a friend of mine, has a government-paid day care center. As far as I understand she works at a job and she is the only supporter and she has two dependents, so she works full time and makes okay money. And she's been working like for eight years now. But the thing is she can't afford day care either, with all of her car insurance, other bills and things like that. So she got this government day care where they have these private homes and you send your child like for an hour before school and it's around your area, that's the way I understand it. And like for the hour or two hours between their ending of school and the mother's work hours. I'm not sure if they take his age, but I'm hoping they do. Now she only pays like $15.00 to $20.00 for this full-time service. It was $20.00 for full time and only $15.00 for part time, which is excellent. You know, I could afford to pay that if I was working.

There is no point in presenting still more quotations from our interviews with young mothers on public assistance to underscore what by now must be evident—that finding satisfactory day care facilities at an affordable price was perhaps the single largest barrier to their succeeding in escaping from welfare, once they determined that that was the way in which they wanted to go. But we must quickly add that for the vast majority who needed to enter into and complete a training program so as to acquire saleable occupational skills, that challenge also presented a formidable hurdle.

A second important barrier to training arises from the fact that training is usually provided under private sector auspices with varying degrees of financial aid made available primarily by the federal government in the form of loans repayable after the completion of the course and subsequent employment.

People on public assistance are loath to take on heavy debts for fear that they may not be able to finish the program successfully or may encounter difficulties in getting a job that would pay enough to enable them to repay their advances within a reasonable period of time. Further, depending on their circumstances, the program, and the administrative rules governing student loans, even those who might have been willing to take the risk were frequently declared ineligible to receive the loan.

In answer to our interviewer's question of whether she had ever been in training before, here is a reply that we elicited:

> I joined this school _____. I don't know if you are familiar with it. But like I say, you have to have a grant, a bank loan, you know. You had to have money. And I had worked a part-time job at the time and it still wasn't enough because I had to have my own place. I was in for five months in the training, but I was denied the grant. They kept saying I was gonna get it, but I never did. It was a good program, but I just couldn't afford it.

Or another interviewee: "You see I was going to _____ Institute and they say it was a rip-off because you had to pay $4,475 for one year. They give you student loans and whatever. So the case worker said that was too much money for one year, for four nights and three hours a day. So I just dropped it. I should have listened to other people though, before that, because they said it wasn't good."

The cost of many preparatory programs in vocational and technical schools and their quality left a great deal to be desired. But the interviewees also reported negatively on many of their experiences with publicly funded programs to which they had had varying degrees of exposure. They complained about teachers who weren't really interested in teaching; about being asked to learn a great many things that they already knew from their former work experience; about entering and completing programs that often failed to provide them with the skills that the employer wanted—at least they had been able to get a job even though they had completed the course.

Then there were such additional difficulties as their having little or no choice in the training that was being offered to them; or the difficulty they faced in getting their carfare and other incidental expenses such as lunch covered.

And then there was an interviewee who alerted us to the reason so many who start training tend to drop out. She saw "embarrassment" as the precipitating cause.

They just stopped coming because they were too embarrassed because they didn't know certain things. She was embarrassed to say like on my resume I put down that I hadn't worked for two years and she didn't know exactly what to say or how to say the reason she hadn't worked for two years. And she was a little bit embarrassed about it. And then she was embarrassed about being on public assistance but that doesn't make me feel embarrassed because I've chosen that form of income. Listen, what you gonna do? You have this child to support and you gotta do something.

We know from recent research that young minority women who have one child out of wedlock and who manage to finish high school have a good chance of not being trapped permanently on welfare. What we have tended to ignore or minimize are the many serious hurdles that such young women face once they decide that remaining on welfare is not for them and that they need a job and an income if they and their child are to have a worthwhile future. The young women whom we interviewed emphasized beyond all other considerations that major barriers in their path resulted from the absence of subsidized, or free, child care facilities and the many weaknesses in the training infrastructure, proprietary and public, from excessive tuition costs to short-term courses that failed to provide them with a marketable skill. The challenge of assuring their employability or reemployability has less to do with their willingness to work and much more to do with the weakness or absence of the transitional assistance which they require to turn their work goals into a reality.

4

Profiles of Unemployed Adult Men

This chapter begins with the interview of Tony, an unemployed black man of twenty-five, followed by interviews with the director and a staff member of one of the best-run PIC referral agencies in Philadelphia, half of whose clients are black men in their mid-twenties to mid-thirties, although some are considerably older. The juxtaposition between the interview of the unemployed man seeking help and the experience of the agency in seeking to assist this clientele goes far to explain both the successes and the limitations of the PIC employment-training efforts. In the commentary at the end of the chapter, attention is directed to the critical factors that make assistance to this group of unemployed persons particularly difficult.

Tony, 25

"I heard about this place from the television. I saw an ad on the screen with a number and I called and then came down here."

(Q) Have you ever been in a training program?

"I'm in a training program right now. Well, yes, I have—no. Wait, the reason why I'm hesitating, I'm not lying. Come to think of it, I was in a couple of training programs. I was in a welding training program, and I dropped out because I was afraid of the financial problems. One thing, if I don't get the job there after I finish all that training, I gotta pay them all that money back. It was $600.00 or so."

(Q) Was the program itself difficult?

"No, it was alright."

(Q) Why did you drop out of the program?

"Well, I dropped out because I was afraid of the financial problems."

(Q) What were you guaranteed as a wage? Do you remember?

"Yeah, it came to about $12.00 an hour, something like that. It was over $900.00 a week I know that."

(Q) Should the government guarantee everybody a job who wants to work?

"A lot of people say they want to work but they ain't gonna work, you know what I'm saying? They like don't really wanna work. If they can prove they wanna work and wanna go out there and get training and everything, yeah, and stay with it, and really stay with it, yeah, I think they should be given a job."

(Q) Do you think the government should make sure every family has enough money to live on?

"It all depends if they working for it. No."

(Q) Do you think people are on welfare because they can't find enough work to support their families?

"Naw. I believe most people are on there because they are lazy. And you know, some are lazy, some are trying to get over. Some even have more kids so they can get on it. Some of these girls, they be getting on with these kids. Just stupid, man. They will get on and to get more money they have another baby. And then when they make the third kid or the fourth kid, they [Philadelphia County Assistance Office (PCAO)] ain't supporting that fourth kid. They support the first three, but the fourth one they say forget about it."

(Q) Do you have a job right now?

"No, but I'm going for training. That's why I have to learn this stuff right here. (He showed me a card with multiplication, addition, and subtraction on it.) Well I can do this—but not all that decimal points and all that stuff. I gotta start practicing, I know that. I know I got to go back to school there and after they train me I hope I can get my job back. The training won't be here, it will be at some place called _____ —or some shit like that."

(Q) Do you think you can get a job after you finish training?

"The ones that's got a high school diploma or been in the Army can. Because, like my brother, he's been in the Army and it's a good possibility that he will get a job easier than somebody who didn't finish high school and like that. And those that don't have no good reference and most of the time they gonna work their butt off and train real hard and they don't get no job after that. So they in trouble all the way around."

(Q) How much influence do your family or friends have on whether you work or look for work?

"I think my family they start nagging me, you know. They say stuff like, you gonna sit home all day, or all your life, don't never have no job. You should get out, and like that. My brother he be saying, 'Tony don't pay no rent, why should I pay rent?' You know. And Tony don't have no job and I'm sure if he had a job he'd be paying to stay here. You know I'm damn near twenty-six years old and I gotta get a job sooner or later. You know. When the lady here told me that she's gonna put me in a training program I said that's decent because I got a better chance of getting a job in a training program than if I just go and fill out an application. It will be a better job too. You know what I'm saying? It won't be like a minimum wage or nothing. It will be pretty good. It should be $200 something a week, something like that. Construction workers they make pretty good money!"

(Q) What would you expect to get paid an hour on a job?

"I would like to make double the minimum wage. Like minimum wage is about $4.00. I guess about $8.25. Something like that."

(Q) Did you have any choice in the type of training you are getting?

"Some schools are like that they have different kinds of things you can join. They say you can take this or that. This particular place where I did the welding training only had welding, but they had different kinds of welding; they had maintenance welding, pipe fitting welding, and I was in a different type welding program than a lot of other guys because I didn't have no high school diploma, and they did. They were in pipe fitting welding or something. I was just in maintenance and all of that.

"Welding is a good job, but I couldn't afford to take the chance on not being able to pay that money back. I couldn't take a chance, man. He said I could pay like $50.00 a week, right? The guy was explaining, you know. He said $50.00 a week, you could pay that off in no time. But at the time I didn't know I was gonna get the job or not. When I had to go take the test, right? I didn't know whether I was gonna fail. Some guys you know, they go out and take the test and they fail, you know, because they get panicky, then they gotta go back to welding school.

"I'm not married but I wish I was. I don't wanna live in sin and do what everybody else do. I'm gonna get married, because that's something that I wanna do. I wanna make three kids. I am looking towards a job now. I mean I can't support three kids without a job.

"I've had a full-time job before but I didn't stay on it. One time I was on this job around _____ Street. But I was around there and this lady gave me a job and I was just standing around the store and she say she needed a new boy to work there for her. So she said come in the morning and I'll give you an interview. So I can see if I can use you or not. So I came there the next morning and she gave me a job. And I stayed there a couple of months, right? And her nephew worked there and she wanted me to do her nephew's work. And I couldn't do her nephew's work, man, and she kept nagging me, you know. She kept saying, 'Do you want this job? Do you want this job? I can get other people to work here.' She kept nagging me, 'Do you want this job or not?' She would say, 'I don't want no boy like you.' She kept harassing me on the job, you know. I just say forget it. I needed a job bad then and I said to myself should I hang in here or what. Not real bad like I was gonna die or something, but I needed it to go out and dress good. I had to take the girls out. You know you can't ask no girl out if you don't have no money."

(Q) Would you rather have a job or be on welfare?

"That's a dumb question, man. I would rather have a job, man, really."

(Q) Do you think this PIC Referral Center should help with child care arrangements?

"Well, it would be nice, but they don't gotta, you know."

(Q) Do you think PIC referral centers should help people with counseling in their personal affairs?

"It would be nice if they did, but they would need more money for that."

The View of a PIC Referral Center Director

"Most of my clients for employment are black Americans. Some are still in school so I can't really serve them. But the rest are maybe seventeen-, eighteen-year olds up to the sixties, but I'd say the majority of people are mid-twenties to mid-thirties.

"So if they're interested in a job or training, the telephone operator will tell them to come in anytime to fill out the application. So people can come in, they fill out our own application, the PIC application, and I think now I've added the EDT form which is the state's eligibility form. I hate doing it, but I give them all three of the forms when they walk in the door."

(Q) How long does that take them?

"Depending on the person . . . a lot of people cannot fill out an application. What happens then is they leave their application with the receptionist. She then gives them a slip of paper telling them to call the next day for an appointment. In order to have the interview with me they have to bring the necessary papers for verifying income, if they have an income, or, if they're on welfare, the welfare part. If they're working or have been working within the last six months, the last three paycheck stubs. If they're not working at all, not receiving welfare, perhaps living with their parents, that gets very involved.

"A lot of young men are not receiving welfare because it only covers, I think, three months, till after the age of forty-five or something. So they bring a list of the jobs they've done in the last six months, the dates, how much they received, then they sign it. It has to be notarized. PIC was notarizing them if they went that far in the process. So anyway, they'd bring all this information with them. They also have to have something to prove that they have the right to work. These are all the government requirements, birth certificate, alien registration card.

"As you see, people are walking in the door and they're running into all of this. Before they even get any kind of help. I didn't used to do it that way. But because of DNRs [Do Not Respond], I decided to make it a little difficult in the beginning. Because I've found that the people who don't go through that are not going to come to the point where they go to the job interview.

"So after they fill out all those papers, they get the paperwork from the receptionist telling them to call for an appointment the following day. I won't give them the appointment the same day. Another step. Another test.

"Okay, so they call the next day, if they call, for an appointment and then, say we'll give them an appointment. I will usually schedule six people at 9:30 and six people at 2:30. Everyone at the same time. So at 9:30, six people are scheduled. The average, three will show up.

"So that's why I decided to go to the one time and let people wait, and it's really no problem if the person is interested. So then, when they come to the interview, they sit down with me, and I go over the information on the application, and I ask them, do they have their documentation that they were supposed to bring? Usually, some people who are used to it, have it all. People who are, say, on welfare, they usually have everything. And they are much easier to deal with because they have a welfare card that covers just about every category. The other people who have been working bring paycheck stubs. I have to figure out income and it's difficult for me—what exactly fits requirements. Because what they do is they take what a person made in the last six months, six months back from today, and they double it for their yearly income. So, you know, it's very difficult for people to understand that, including myself. That's what I do.

"But once anyone is sitting here, I help them anyway. But I do get all of those documents and then we continue with the interview. Before they leave, I take a xerox of everything and I put it in their folder.

"So then I go through the application. I might ask some people I sit down with—'why are you here?'

"You'll have people coming in looking wild—a guy in shorts, mirrored sunglasses, a headband, 'I want a job.' Oh—do you? Have you ever looked for a job before because you're not going to get one looking like that.

"This particular person I remember had had experience in auto mechanics, diesel mechanics. He was a good candidate. He was a DNR, by the way. I called him in later. I got a job notice from PIC for a diesel mechanic, very rare, and he was very rare. So I called him up, he came in, still had on the glasses. I told him look, you have to dress. I even have a little copy of how to dress for an interview for men and women which I sometimes just offer to them. Because that's very important.

"Okay, what happens next? So I go over the application with them, point out inconsistencies, you know, dates, times, the way they filled out the applications—and ask them questions why they left the job, and, you know, other questions, which takes about forty minutes, not all, 'cause you tease it out now, 'cause you're skilled at it. I would tell them look, I'm not the guy hiring. You can tell me. So they'll tell me then. Usually.

"And then, okay, the majority of the people I'm interviewing are not highly skilled, they're not really job ready, the majority have no skills. So what I'll do is I'll start. Say somebody really wants a job. I'll say, well, do you have a driver's license? And there's no driver's license. Too bad. This job has driving. Or a steady work history. You haven't had a job more than five months. In the last ten years. And that's pretty common. They'll take a job for a couple months and then quit it. Or get fired. So you can't really go for that job either.

"Yesterday a guy came in here who was referred to me by a person I had placed in psychiatric technician training last year, so he is working as a psych technician. It was nice to hear that because that was someone who didn't know what he wanted to do and then he went into this psychiatric position, after talking to me about what his options were at that time.

"What happens if someone comes in and says look I need a real job with real money? I will say well we do have welding, electrical welding training, which begins at eight something an hour and you can make $13.00 an hour within a year. So that's very attractive to men who have some interest in that kind of thing. And I say, do you use any drugs? Coke? Grass? I say, you may as well tell me. You're going to be tested. And you will not be accepted into the program if you use any drugs.

"Now it's, no, nothing, nothing—Oh, my God, I think, what was the percentage? It was something outrageous. I think it was like 70 percent of the people who got as far as the interview with the training department. Oh it was outrageous. They can get the exact number.

"This one guy who tested positive for coke, I said you don't even have to give it up—all you have to do is not be doing it for two days. They [the employers] start to overlook grass. Okay we'll live with it. But the coke we can't take.

"And it was an outrageous number. That program took months to get started because of the drug problem. And I mean if someone wants this training, if someone wants the training, it's real easy, because then they know what they want to do and I can tell them what's available and [find out] if they're interested in it and they have the circumstances where they can afford not to have money coming in or, you know, they have that kind of personality that they will deal with some hardship in order to develop a skill."

The View of PIC Referral Center Staff

(Q) I'm really curious about why the Center works, why you have low DNR rates. What is it about your approach that makes this operation work?

"I'm very tough, and people who don't like to work with me, because I'm tough, they don't come back. The people who really want to work with me, I'm willing to work with them too. I feel that that's the reason. Like when I see a client for the first time and I make the assessment and I try to figure out what they need. And if a client needs a training program but is not really ready for a training program either. We have here a two-week training program where we prepare them for jobs. I tell them we are going to have to work with them, but it's gonna have to be fifty-fifty. We will work with them, but they will have to come to a two-week training program and then if they complete it, good, they go to the second step. So maybe forty people that I tell to come to a two-week training program, only ten come. From the ten that come they have to come here for a two-week training program. And then I have the opportunity to talk to them and see them and then they are more motivated to go on to a training program."

(Q) Do you have a very rigid approach to the training? What is the time that you do the training?

"Well, we do the training from eight in the morning until twelve noon. And then they are free for the rest of the day. We give them two tokens a day so they have the transportation. I'm not the person that runs the program. This is a very big agency."

(Q) What you have then is a built-in commitment quotient. People who come to you must be motivated to finish the training and take a job. Is that right?

"We try and weed out those who don't want to come to training. Sometimes I have clients who don't need training. You know, like this girl. I saw her yesterday and I made her come today again, so I can see if she really wants to come. If she wants to do it, fine. I'm here and we are going to do it together. If you don't want to do it, there is nothing I can do. I didn't call her or anything. But I know she wants to go through the training program because I see her motivation."

(Q) Could you tell me what the demographics of your organization are?

"Most of the clients that come here are citywide. This is an agency that is citywide. Most of our people are black people; we have white people; we have about 80 percent black, 10 percent white, 10 percent Latin."

(Q) What percentage are women?

"We have about 50 percent women."

(Q) What percentage are welfare mothers?

"About 90 percent of the mothers are welfare."

(Q) Are any of those males on welfare? What qualifies those males to be on welfare?

"They are not unemployed, but we work with drug clients when they are in the rehabilitation center. To be in the rehabilitation center they have to be in the PCAO."

(Q) Are these males married?

"Yes, some of them. Some of them are single, but most of them have children. I would say less than half of them are married but with kids."

(Q) As you look at what you're doing here and you project over the next one or two years, what do you see your population being?

"I know because I did that study. Now in New York and Philadelphia there is a short labor supply. There are jobs available but there are no people. So what's happening now is the people that don't have skills are around in these programs. And I can't do much for them because most of them don't want to come to a two-week training program. Because they feel they don't need it and they don't have the energy or the motivation to come to a two-week program. So what I see now is like a circle and that circle is closed. Jobs are available, but employers they don't wanna hire the kind of people that are looking for work. And these people they don't wanna go to the training programs either. That's why I speak to them here because I want to train those people and find them a job. But they don't wanna go to a training program."

(Q) You have a wide-lensed look. You have a look that I'm trying to capture. What would make training more attractive for people to come in?

"I think we need to do more advertisement. The advertisement would bring in more people, but the advertisement would tell them more about the training programs and what would be good about the training programs. Like in the clerical training program we have to type twenty words a minute. These are people who want to go into the training program, but they don't type twenty words a minute. Like pretty soon we are gonna have a warehouse training program and I hope it is going to attract a lot of people."

(Q) What would that training program involve?

"It is a basic entry-level position in the warehouse field. And we hope it will be the easiest training program to start."

(Q) Something turns people off from training. People are saying I'd rather not work than go through this training program. Why is that? What do you see as the reason?

"I don't think it is because of the training program. The client who comes here, he has a personality, he has a background, and maybe he's tired. He has his own problems. He may think, oh, no, here's another training program and I'm not gonna find a job. They think that."

(Q) So you need to build in a kind of trust factor in the whole process?

"We do that because here we are very open and very candid. The clients come here after they have jobs and everything. We have graduates who come to the two-week training who have jobs and they tell the people in training they have jobs and everything. Also when they get hired we have a big sign that says this person got hired and we have certificates outside. Like I said before, people get hired all throughout the training program. And before they got there they receive a lot of phone calls from their friends, so their friends hear about it and they come too."

(Q) You do training here and you send people out for training, is that right? Could you explain that part of your system to me?

"The two-week training program, we do it here. But like when they have like a clerical training program they go to different training providers. That's PIC. We receive a training notice when the training is going to start, where it is going to start, and all the qualifications. And the client comes and he wants to go to that training program. First I test them here to be sure that they qualify. And then if they qualify they fill out the PIC application and we send them to the training program provider."

(Q) Do they have to pay for this training?

"PIC pays them a stipend of $35.00 a week or $7.00 a day so they can go to the training program. This is transportation money, etc. The training program provider is going to get paid from PIC when each person is placed. They have to place 75 percent of those people."

(Q) How much are the training providers paid per person?

"I think they are paid $500.00 per person. PIC pays us per client: $150.00 for the first thirty placements and the thirty-first we get $250.00. And then we [the center] get a bonus of $1,000."

(Q) Do you know about the state programs?

"A little bit, not too much. I start to trust PIC. I know the clients can be placed. Because I see the results. But the clients, they don't trust. Believe me, we had a study here, like last month I sent out 240 applications and in September I set up 227 interviews for the whole month and only eighty people came. So there you have the first cause of DNR. And from those eighty people maybe forty are going to be referred to the other program. And out of those forty maybe fifteen comes. I think what the other agencies do is send the people to the interviews right away. They don't let them be screened, or say like I do, make them come back here and sometimes that happens to me and I realize that's no good. Because we want people only if they are motivated. The other places I assume just send people to the training programs or to the jobs and they just don't show up. If I see a client and he's perfect for the job and I like him and everything, I say come in the afternoon or come the next day. Sometimes they come, sometimes they don't come."

Commentary

It is important to emphasize that many unemployed men in their mid-twenties to mid-thirties have some combination of the following characteristics and experiences: they dropped out of high school; their arithmetic and writing skills are exceedingly limited—that is they are likely to lack the ability to handle fractions which may be a prerequisite for carrying out quite simple blue-collar work; and their work record is full of holes, a reflection of the fact that during the past decade or more they seldom if ever held down a full-time job, at least for any length of time. Employers, even if short of labor, are understandably disinclined to add an adult man to their payrolls whose work record over the past decade reveals that he has spent much more time out of work than in work.

But these men, even though their prior work records have been spotty, and they may have acquired certain behavior patterns often including the use of drugs, still have strong views about the job market. They have views as to what they are entitled to if they get a job—"double the minimum wage"; they see certain types of work as "women's work" and shy away from it; they may have run into harassment from employers in previous jobs, as Tony reports; or they started out in proprietary training but dropped out for fear that they would be unable to pay off their debts if, at the end of the course, they failed to qualify and did not obtain a job. A substantial number of these men have children, although they have not been married; and many of them have had exposure to the drug trade and encounters with the police.

Many of them recognize that it is important for them to acquire a skill in order to get a regular job, without which they will be unable to marry and bring up a family, but there is a wide divide between their perception of the importance of regular work and a regular income and their ability to turn their goal into a reality.

The interviews with the training center director and the staff member who work on a daily basis with a large number of these unemployed, unskilled men (as well as with a large number of mothers on welfare) provide additional perspective in operating a bridge institution whose goal is to facilitate the transition of this disadvantaged group into employment. The points that come through their answers to our interviewer's probing questions included the following. Getting into a training program requires the applicant to run an obstacle course. He must be able to fill out not one but several applications and personal statements and present supporting documents to establish his eligibility. Even with considerable staff assistance, this is no small hurdle for men who have long led inactive lives and whose primary relationship to the world of work has been in the "off-the-record" economy where the absence of records is the distinguishing characteristic. Some who have had brushes with the police and who may have served time are reluctant to attest to such events on the assumption that it will only make their future adjustment even more complicated.

Once they apply to the Center they confront something that is basically alien to their way of life. They are given not one but several opportunities to "test their motivation." This means that they must show on time, sit around and wait their turn and then answer a lot of probing questions. All of these requirements are in varying degrees discouraging, the more so because many of them know from personal experience or from their friends and acquaintances that even those who get into a training program and stay the course are not certain to get a job and surely not a job that will last and provide them with the opportunity to move up.

But the staff believes that it has no option but to act tough up-front and to make each applicant undergo a "motivational" test by requiring that they appear at the scheduled interviews. In the absence of proof that they are really serious about training and a job, these men will never stay the course. As the staff member pointed out, after having set up over 200 interviews to identify likely candidates for a training program, the net yield at the end of successive losses during the processing amounted to fifteen!

Not every center follows this careful preliminary screening, motivational approach. Many send applicants out for a job interview, not once but repeatedly, just as soon as they have completed the minimum paperwork. But as the interviews with the director and the staff member record, they saw little or no point to such a churning effort. In their view an applicant who doesn't know how to dress will never get past the employment office. And they also believe that with few exceptions their long-term unemployed with at best a thin work record need all or most of the information, attitudinal and behavior cues that are provided during the two-week orientation training. Yet the staff recognizes that many of the unemployed balk at this training and they lose out because of it.

There is little point in trying to calculate the extent to which the successes and limitations of the employment-training efforts directed at long-term unemployed adult men reflect their successive developmental deficits and defeats and to what extent it reveals weaknesses in program structure and implementation. The important point that the interviews reveal is that some of these men who would like to escape from their long-term marginal status of a life without regular work are seldom able to mobilize their resources from within themselves to accomplish this task; and that the extant system is at best only modestly structured to meet their multiple and diverse needs for assistance.

5

Labor Market and Other Barriers

The preceding three chapters have explored the problem of employability primarily from the vantage point of the individual who is seeking a job or, less frequently, is being pressured by family or the welfare worker to look for one. We find that most unemployed persons, after they have confronted the negatives connected with unemployment in terms of little or nothing to do month after month and year after year, sooner or later miss the freedom and satisfaction that come with having money of one's own. At that point, they look positively on the benefits of working and supporting oneself and one's dependents.

Labor Market Barriers

The last three chapters focused on the personal characteristics of the unemployed and their family needs—primarily day care services—that made it difficult or impossible for many to make the transition from unemployment and/or welfare to self-supporting job.

But the circumstances of the person seeking work is only one side of the problem. The other side is the demand for workers as expressed by employers in the private and, to a lesser extent, in the public sector. The high unemployment levels of 1981–1982 meant that nearly one out of every ten persons who was looking for work was unable to find it. In mid-1988 the proportion had dropped to just over one in twenty. This radical shift within a six-year period underscores the fact that unemployment cannot be assessed solely in terms of the characteristics of the unemployed but must also consider the demand for labor in specific labor markets. While it is true that over long periods of time persons of working age located in areas of high unemployment will relocate to areas where the job outlook is more favorable, such relocations are inherently difficult (leaving family and friends and finding housing in the new location) and significant shifts usually occur only after a number of years.

But there are many more problems on the demand side. To mention the most important: sectoral changes in the economy from the manufacture of goods to the production of services; the differentiation between jobs based on gender, with many categories overwhelmingly filled by women; the shift of jobs within metropolitan areas, with many or most of the additions taking place in the suburbs rather than in the central city; the extent to which racism and discriminatory behavior continues to characterize the behavior of employers; and the transportation-housing infrastructures that can do so much to facilitate or retard the matching of the unemployed in search of a job with employers who have jobs to fill.

We will briefly discuss each of the above factors that has influenced and continues to influence the extent to which the Philadelphia PIC has been able to assist the unemployed and those outside of the labor market in finding a job.

The single most important change in the Philadelphia labor market within the last three years has been the marked reduction in the unemployment rate, from 8.1 percent in 1985 to 5 percent in 1988. Such a pronounced tightening of the labor market has a series of impacts on both the number who seek assistance from the PIC as well as the attitude and behavior of the employer community in using the PIC as a supporting source of workers.

The PIC staff was surprised in the summer of 1987 to find that it was encountering difficulties in filling all of its Phil-A-Job openings. In previous summers the number of applicants had consistently exceeded the number of slots available. Inquiry disclosed that a large number of young people in 1987 were able to locate summer jobs on their own and in many instances fared better than on a Phil-A-Job.

The steady tightening of the Philadelphia labor market over the last several years has meant that a declining number and proportion of potential workers have sought assistance from PIC. They have been able, with the help of their family and friends, to make it into the world of work. In time, PIC has been left to deal with the residual population distinguished by multiple employment deficits.

It is a well-recognized phenomenon that employers tend to modify their hiring requirements in response to the looseness or tightness of the labor market. That means that over the last few years they have been more willing to take a chance on a job applicant who has some shortcomings and disabilities, but none so serious as to preclude his or her becoming a satisfactory employee.

Philadelphia, like other principal East Coast cities, including Boston, New York, and Baltimore, has been in the throes of a transformation that has moved its economy out of manufacturing into more and more output of services. This process has had a pronounced and differential impact on the potential of poorly educated men and women to obtain and retain jobs. Manufacturing was the classic entrance job for a sizable proportion of all high school dropouts. The shift of the local economy away from manufacturing to services has added immeasurably to the difficulties that poorly educated young men face in gaining a toehold in the job market.

The expansion of service employment has resulted in a heightened demand for new workers who have numeracy and literacy skills. Aside from such important negatives as the fact that many black men look upon office work as "female" work and shy away from it, and further are disenchanted with such jobs because they tend to pay considerably less than a regular "male" job in manufacturing or construction, there is the environmental factor that must be considered. Office work places a premium on dress, speech, and social interaction in place of the much more informal atmosphere on the factory floor with its roughhousing, camaraderie, physical exertion—all "he-man" activities. There is no question that the sectoral shift in the Philadelphia economy has had and continues to have an adverse effect on the employability of male dropouts and even graduates from high school.

The obverse of this negative trend for men has been the expanded opportunity that the growth in service production has provided for women. For the sizable number of women who have obtained their high school diplomas—and even for some who dropped out in the eleventh or twelfth year—there has been a steadily expanding number of office and other service jobs. In Philadelphia today, eight out of ten jobs are service jobs and this ratio is expected to increase to nine out of ten.

Although the United States has made considerable progress in lowering the discriminatory barriers to employment, the Philadelphia labor market, like all large labor markets, is characterized by employer preferences for native-born white men, followed by white women, the foreign born, with blacks and Hispanics usually at the end of the queue. This is not a rigid ordering since employer requirements and worker skills can enable one or another of the less-favored groups to advance in the queue, but by and large the ordering tends to hold over most of the available job offerings.

When one recalls that about two out of every five persons living in Philadelphia are black, the significance of employer preferences for white workers weighs heavily on the black minority in search of jobs.

Minority workers face a further hurdle by virtue of the fact that Philadelphia is a heavily unionized city and in many jobs with preferred wages and working conditions, unions are able to determine within wide margins whom they will admit to apprenticeship or to journeymen jobs. In many instances such jobs are handed down from father to son or uncle to nephew. In any case, the more distant a young person growing up is from union members, the less his prospects for breaking in. The construction trades, despite court orders to admit more minorities, may have complied with the letter but surely not with the spirit of the law.

As is the case in all large urban communities, city government controls a sizable number of jobs, circa 26,500 in Philadelphia or about 3.4 percent of total employment within the city. Many of these jobs are beyond the reach of the PIC constituency because they require professional or technical training, and a great many others are assigned on the basis of the applicant's relative score on a test which is beyond the capacity of many, if not most, of the hard-to-employ. The remainder of the city jobs tend to be distributed among the chieftains of the local political party that is in control of city government, a group of influentials with whom the hard-to-employ have few, if any, close contacts.

There is no need to belabor further the adverse effects of racism, discrimination, and lack of political connections on the job prospects of the hard-to-employ. But reference should be made to a widespread attitude of many, though fortunately not all, employers that also tends to restrict further the job opportunities of persons applying to and receiving services from the PIC. The fact that a man or woman has sought out such services and has received them is viewed by some employers as presumptive evidence that he or she has certain weaknesses in education, skills, or work experience. Hence many employers (and their personnel departments) shy away from tapping into this labor source. However, there is a compensatory factor at work. An employer who has had one or more positive experiences with the graduates of PIC programs, has hired some of them, and has found that they perform effectively is likely to seek additional graduates when adding workers to the payroll. But since the number of employers that have made use of the PIC is far fewer than those without firsthand experience, the critical views of the business community toward the clients of governmentally sponsored programs must be seen as still one additional barrier that confronts the hard-to-employ in their job-seeking efforts.

Up to this point the discussion about job seekers and jobs has focused exclusively on the city proper. But in point of fact the labor market extends beyond the city limits and encompasses an ever larger number of new and more distant suburban areas. While the central city of Philadelphia has been experiencing a considerable turnaround with much new construction and job expansion, especially in the area of business services and finance, considerably more economic growth has taken place in the outlying areas, beyond the borders of the city.

The statement that the greatest job growth in the Philadelphia area has taken place beyond the city's boundaries, of and by itself, does not tell us a great deal about the impact of this trend on the large number of hard-to-employ who are city residents. Clearly, where people live and where the job openings are expanding puts a special focus on the availability and cost of transportation, both in terms of dollars and time. And it also raises the issue of the ease or difficulty that the city population would face if it sought to shift its residence from the inner city to the near or outer suburbs.

The term "mainliner" has achieved idiomatic status in the evolution of the United States, conveying the fact that the affluent and the wealthy in the Philadelphia area have long lived in a series of communities along the main line of the commuter railroad that connects the places where they live with the places where they go to work in the morning and from which they return at the end of the day.

While some minority persons live within a reasonable distance of the main commuting lines, the largest concentrations are located some considerable distance away, which requires them to make use of three different transportation systems to get from their homes in the inner city to a job in the suburbs—from home to their town station in Philadelphia, town to the suburbs, and from the suburban station to their employer. On average, the commute both ways would come close to three hours, allowing for waiting time, and the daily cost to a suburb neither close by nor far out and would cost about $7.60 per day, or $95.00 per month, taking into account the reduced cost for a monthly ticket. This means that transportation alone, without the cost of lunch, would represent over 10 percent of an employee's starting wage. It would also mean that a so-called eight-hour day would stretch into an eleven-hour day.

But this schematic account of what a daily commute to a job in the suburbs implies fails to reflect one remaining hurdle: How does the commuter from the city obtain transportation from the suburban town station to his or her employer's locale? While some employers, recognizing the problem, have arranged bus transportation, others do not have sufficient flows of city-based workers to justify the expense and do not provide shuttle service which means that the worker must make his own way on the last lap, which is a challenge that many are unable to solve.

There have been on-again and off-again discussions between the public transportation authorities, suburban employers, and city officials aimed at developing new approaches to easing the transportation of inner-city workers to suburban locations. Progress has been slow, but two new routes are now operating—the first to the Corporate Park in

Malvern, and the second to the Fort Washington Industrial Park. The wide dispersion of companies over the outer areas makes it very difficult, even with extensions of the railroad lines and improved bus connections, to develop the minimum volume of users that would justify the capital expenses involved and assure that the operating expenses would be covered.

Even with substantial federal subsidies that were made available to improve the linkage between the people living in the Watts area of Los Angeles and the expanding labor markets beyond the Los Angeles limits, no practical solution was ever developed and most of the subsidized efforts folded before long.

If the transportation hurdle cannot be overcome, that leaves but one other solution on the drawing board and that would be for smaller or larger numbers of the inner-city population to obtain housing in one or another of the suburbs which were experiencing a substantial growth in jobs. While such a solution has proved feasible for a small number of managerial and professional minority workers in the middle and higher income ranges, especially in two-worker families, the cost of suburban housing makes it a totally unrealistic alternative for most hard-to-employ minority persons.

The thrust of the foregoing analysis has been to call attention to major trends in the labor market that place major hurdles in the path of the hard-to-employ who are seeking regular jobs. Admittedly, the modest educational backgrounds, limited skills, and restricted work experience of many or even most of the job seekers go far to explain their difficulties in getting and holding a job. But the burden of this analysis has been to call attention to a number of characteristics of the larger society that individually and collectively represent major barriers to a successful job search.

A quick reminder: The shift of the economy toward services has eliminated a large number of entry-level positions in manufacturing, a major route into work for many minority males. The persistence of racism and other forms of discrimination in the labor market present special hurdles to minority persons in search of jobs. And the fact that so much of the job growth in recent years has been in the outlying suburban areas rather than in the city proper has added to the employment problems of the inner-city population because of inadequate or nonexistent transportation networks. And the relocation of the urban minority poor to these areas is a nonstarter given the cost of housing in the outlying regions, aside from all the social barriers.

The growth of cities in the nineteenth and early decades of the twentieth centuries was predicated on the economic gains from the ready availability of a large number of potential workers. The automobile in juxtaposition with the preference of many, in fact most, Americans to own their home led to suburbanization and urban sprawl. It is by no means clear, as the twentieth century enters its last decade, that the focus on decentralization may not be creating new costs for suburbanites that will lead to a new configuration of residences and jobs. But in the interim it is clear that the low-income population trapped in the inner city is at a particular disadvantage as it seeks to obtain and maintain a toehold in the world of work.

Other Barriers

In addition to the conditions imbedded in labor markets that adversely affect the employability of the hard-to-employ, there are institutional barriers within the PIC referral-training structures that warrant brief consideration. In this section we consider why persons who initially contact PIC fail to follow through and look more closely at a number of major PIC trainers to see what they have to offer prospective clients and the special efforts they make to help them find permanent jobs.

The "Do Not Respond" (DNR) Problem

Both the Philadelphia PIC and the PIC Referral Centers have been plagued with the problem posed by the lack of follow-through by potential clients who at some stage in the job training/job placement process fail to keep appointments and drop out. The "do not respond" (DNR) problem has marked every stage, from initial interview after contact has been made to the final stage when it is necessary to start a job. The dropout rate by adults and young people alike is assumed to be at least 50 percent.

To obtain a clearer understanding of the reasons for this phenomenon, the researchers, with the assistance and active support of the PIC staff, secured the cooperation of the PIC Referral Centers (PRCs) in filling out a special form to pinpoint the stage at which the DNR occurred, the possible reasons, the age and sex of the persons involved, and the age of the youngest child. This form was to be completed for all who made contact in search of training or employment over a specified two-week period in the summer of 1988. Two-thirds of the PRCs completed the survey.

DNR: Stage One. A total of 319 DNRs failed to appear at the first stage for the interview that was set after they had walked in off the street or telephoned to request an appointment. The failure to appear, of course, made it impossible to elicit the reason for the nonresponse. It was possible, however, to analyze the demographics of this population from information obtained by the PRC staff person, either on the telephone or in person. Such information included name, gender, age, marital status, and age of the youngest child. The last was, of course, particularly important when the applicant was a welfare mother.

Six in ten DNRs were female, four in ten male. When females with preschool children in the household are excluded, there is an almost exactly equal distribution between the sexes.

This was a predominantly under-forty age group with 94 percent of the men and 86 percent of the women in this category. There was some skewing of the female age distribution toward the older ages: only 6 percent of the men, but 14 percent of the women, were over age forty. In fact, two women were over the age of sixty.

Seven in ten of the female DNRs either had no children at home or had a youngest child above the age of six. The remaining three in ten had a preschool child. Although a few became mothers when they were only twelve or thirteen, some continued to attend high school at least for a period of time.

DNR: Stage Two. Of those who did keep the appointment for an interview, a fair number dropped out of the system at that point. The following reasons were given by the five largest PRCs as to why these people "came once, never returned": not interested; poor attitude; failed security clearance; physical problem; very low scores; can't read.

Clearly, many of these reasons are interrelated. It is not difficult to predict that limited literacy and low scores would lead to a "poor attitude" (as well as embarrassment) and lack of interest. Moreover, clients with such characteristics are particularly at risk and are most likely to fall to the bottom in any "creaming" operation in which only those most likely to succeed are chosen for training.

DNR: Stage 3. At this stage clients have made an initial contact, secured an appointment for an interview, have appeared for the interview and assessment and been assigned to either classroom training or an OJT slot, but then fail to appear. The overall rate of DNRs at this stage in the last fiscal year was 27.5 percent, 30 percent for classroom training, and somewhat over 20 percent for OJT.

About half of the PRCs (seventeen out of thirty-seven) reported sixty-three DNRs at the very beginning of this stage of the process. The characteristics of this population are suggestive of possible reasons for their dropping out, not all necessarily negative. There were thirty-seven females and twenty-six males in this group.

At least half of the females were on public assistance, with the rest living at home with parents (the younger group); some were between jobs and living on savings, or, in two cases, were employed but seeking a better job.

Half had preschool children at home. Of those who described their marital status, twenty-six were single, eight married, and one divorced. Two out of three were between the ages of twenty-five and forty-three and seemed to be caught up in the drive to get welfare mothers off the rolls and into training or jobs.

Their educational attainments, prior training, and previous work experience pointed to the possibility of the effort to succeed. Of the thirty-seven, seventeen had a high school diploma or a GED and four had attended community colleges for varying lengths of time. At least ten had had previous training in business subjects, including accounting, nursing assistant, dental assistant, and health aide. In addition, thirty-five of the thirty-seven had some previous work experience, with clerk, cashier, housekeeper, seamstress, and health aide among the most frequently mentioned. One was an ex-offender who had received some training while in jail.

The age distribution of the men was on the whole similar to that of the women, with some skewing to the younger ages. Three out of five were between twenty-five and forty-three, but more males than females were under the age of twenty. All but one male, including those who indicated that they had dependent children, were single. There were four ex-offenders in the group.

Nine had either high school diplomas or a GED and two had had some community college background. In addition, nine had had some type of vocational training, including one who had acquired training as a utility worker while in the Marine Corps.

All indicated that they had previous work experience in a range of occupations considerably wider than that of the females: railway trackman, construction helper, stock clerk, meat packer, dishwasher, security guard, handyman, welder, and prison guard. At the time of the survey seven were on public assistance.

No man or woman reported fewer than two years of high school attendance.

In light of the foregoing, particularly their education and work experience, one can surmise that some part of this group of DNRs found jobs on their own. On average, their somewhat older age suggests a greater impatience with additional formal training.

The DNR survey results are a powerful reminder of the many sources for slippage that exist even after an unemployed person or a person out of the labor force takes the initial step to cross the bridge to work. The slippage can arise from weaknesses within the individual, from unmanageable problems within the household (particularly the care of dependent children), lack of interest or success in the training program, or from still other causes. However, as the following brief descriptions and assessments of the major PIC training procedures' structure and operations help to clarify, clients who get this far in the process and who are able to stay the course are likely to make a successful transition into a permanent job.

Interviews with some of the major classroom and OJT trainers provided additional insights into the dropout-retention picture.

Classroom Trainer 1 is part of a national chain that is the largest clerical trainer in the country and bases its training on the twin principles of positive reinforcement and results-oriented operations. The clients stay in training (within limits) until they get a job, and there is open entry and exit. All of the students are PIC-eligible and the operation is virtually limited to PIC referrals. Training is given in typing, word processing, shorthand, and legal and medical secretarial skills. Only state-of-the-art equipment is used.

The trainees are 90 percent female and mainly black. The males work almost exclusively on word processing which, since a computer is involved, is considered an acceptable male occupation. The average age is twenty-five to twenty-seven and 85 percent of the females are single parents. If the trainees do not have an eighth grade reading level, academic instructors are brought in to provide remediation.

There is a good placement record, helped by the strong demand for trained clericals in the Philadelphia labor market. A great fuss is made about everyone who has a successful interview and gets a job, and they serve as a concrete model for the other clients. The training period spans six to nine months and everyone stays until they get a job. While consistent tardiness is a cause for being dropped from the program, considerable understanding is shown for the problems of the enrollees, including permission, if the baby-sitting arrangement slips, for the mother to bring the young child to class for the day.

The annual put-through is between 200 and 300, and placements average about twenty per month. A follow-up study based on a five-year retention study indicated that 80 percent of the trainees still held a job. Other studies suggest that the dropout rate from the job market is about 8 to 10 percent a year, attributable in good part to poor housing and the disruptive effects of having to move frequently.

One of the most frequent comments made by the trainees who have unsuccessfully attempted to negotiate the financial costs of proprietary schools relates to their amazement that this PIC training is not only free but leads to good jobs.

Classroom Trainer 2 is also part of a national chain and is also PIC-exclusive. The training is for the more male-dominated occupations: photocopier repair, electronics, telecommunications (cable, wiring, phone installation), and is provided by competent professionals. The trainees are mainly male and black, with some Hispanics and Asians, mostly in the eighteen to twenty age group.

Entry tests are given to determine if the applicants are at the eighth grade level in reading and math, and, if not, remediation is provided as well as assistance in getting a GED. The training period for copier repair is fifteen to eighteen weeks and for the others, twelve weeks. Socialization is stressed as well as resumé and letter writing. Classes are eight hours per day, five days per week.

Strong market demand could lead to 100 percent placement since the supply is inadequate to meet the demand. A copier repairer commands a minimum of $200 per week plus benefits and the use of a company car. A problem arises because the young trainees cannot afford a car and Philadelphia insurance is expensive (50 percent of the city's drivers are uninsured), and this fact alone leads to a 20 percent dropout rate from this program. Job placement in telecommunications, though not as remunerative, is easier to negotiate. PIC alone cannot supply a sufficient number of eligible applicants, leading the trainer to do its own advertising and to refer PIC-eligibles who appear to PIC for certification. If the trainee cannot be placed in ninety days, the trainer works with him further until placement.

Classroom Trainer 3 is a health care trainer which has been in existence for thirteen years. The clients are mainly black females in their late twenties, most of whom have either a high school diploma or a GED. Hispanic females are difficult to recruit and retain, and even when programs are taken into their community and jobs are locally available, retention is low.

The types of training offered include EKG/EEG (twelve months), medical records (ten months), pharmacy technician (six months), medical secretary (ten months), third-party billing clerk (seventeen weeks), home health aide (eight weeks), and still others. The more highly technical training is subcontracted to area hospitals.

There is no problem of placement after training, given this trainer's links with area hospitals and home health aide agencies. The largest number of dropouts occurs among welfare mothers. The public assistance case workers are held partly to blame because of their insistence on rigid procedures which require mothers on public assistance to complete required paperwork during class time, making an inherently difficult situation worse.

OJT Employer 1 is a large national food supplier to institutional users, airports, and the like. The types of jobs for which training is provided include food service worker (trained to handle equipment), porter (learn to handle trash compactor, different cleaning solutions, etc.), cook (the most sought after and difficult to obtain), and counter attendant (trained to handle cash registers and operate such equipment as microwave ovens, soda fountains). A few clerical jobs, such as cashier-supervisor and bookkeeper, are also available, with in-house training given to supplement previously acquired training.

Trainees are mainly black and in their late twenties. Wages start at $4.90 per hour, supplemented by meals in the employees' cafeteria, uniforms, a uniform cleaning allowance, and free parking. The training period is six weeks. The retention rate is good and DNR is seldom a problem. When positions become open they are bid for through the local union.

There is general satisfaction with the program and with the PIC relationship.

OJT Trainer 2 is a large hotel with three main types of jobs available: maid ($5.67 per hour), janitor ($5.67 per hour), and chef ($6.49 per hour). The training period is six weeks. Occasionally, other jobs such as night porter, driver, dining room server, and PBX operator also become available. Most trainees complete the training period and the thirty-day probationary period. The firm, however, waits sixty days before making employment permanent, finding that unexplained absences and tardiness are major problems. Those who survive the ninety-day probationary period tend to keep their jobs.

* * *

There are two ways to assess the burden of the foregoing analysis. The first is to see the barriers in the labor market and the institutional difficulties that confront clients in negotiating the PIC process as so intimidating that only the exceptional person can cross the bridge into employment. But a closer view reveals that there is a wide array of training opportunities available to all except the most severely disadvantaged. There are also good support systems during training and effective placement linkages after completion of training. Individuals who can reach that point in the process and stay the training course have the opportunity to cross the bridge into permanent employment.

6

Lessons for Policy:
Local and National

In the twenty-six years since the Manpower Development and Training Act (MDTA) was passed with bipartisan support in the second year of the Kennedy administration, the nation has been directly and continuously involved in employment and training programs for unemployed and hard-to-employ persons. Since most of the federal funds passed through the state and local service delivery agencies, it is fair to say that the entire country has been involved in some degree with programs aimed at improving the employability and employment of a large number of persons with limited skills and other job handicaps.

The administrative structure of this training effort has been modified over the years and the level of congressional funding has undergone major gyrations from an initial appropriation of $52 million in 1962 to a peak allocation of over $11 billion in 1979. More recent annual appropriations for the JTPA have been in the mid-$3 billion range. The cumulative congressional appropriations over the last twenty-six years, disregarding the depreciation of the dollar, approximates $125 billion. An expenditure of this magnitude over a period of more than a quarter of a century should provide a reasonably firm base for valid inferences and deductions about the efficacy of the effort, both from a local and national perspective.

But this presumption must be questioned once one takes note of the following forces: the great variability in the local management and leadership of these programs; the marked differences in the strengths and weaknesses of local economies, which play such a large role in determining the demand for labor; the absence of reliable data; and the lack of analysis of the experiences of clients, in particular whether they were able to retain private sector jobs for more than thirty days, the required follow-up period.

Among the most serious drawbacks has been the low or nonexistent interest of the funders and administrators to look closely at how the target groups perceived and responded to the efforts that were made to assist them—what they found right and wrong about the system which has been put and kept in place to help them move from unemployment or out-of-the labor force to a regular long-term job.

The Philadelphia PIC story reported in this monograph represents a unique effort to focus attention on the attitudes, feelings, behavior, and reactions of three major groups of PIC clients: in-school and out-of-school youth; young mothers on welfare; and unemployed minority adult men. There is no need in this concluding chapter to review the rich material that is contained in the selected interviews presented in Chapters 2, 3, and 4. Rather, the focus here will be on policy lessons from two vantage points: local and national. It should be emphasized again that the JTPA and the Philadelphia PIC, like all federally funded programs, must operate within a number of major constraints, the most important of which are the available dollars; eligibility criteria; performance-based outcomes; and restrictions on use of funds.

Since Congress stipulated that the goal of the program was to assist a significant proportion of all clients placed in training to move into permanent jobs, the Philadelphia PIC, like all other service deliverers, has only limited discretion when it comes to selecting candidates, funding particular training programs, and determining the length of the training period. The implicit, if not explicit, goal is to assist the optimal number of needy persons to meet the goal of obtaining and holding a regular job at the conclusion of training.

Even in the heyday of federal funding in the late 1970s, when Philadelphia had far more to spend on assisting the hard-to-employ than the approximate $25 million current PIC budget, the program administrators faced the dilemma of selecting from the top, the middle, or the lower end of the applicant pool. The lower they went, the less their prospect of success, measured in placing clients in regular jobs. But the JTPA performance standards (a 70 percent "entered" placement rate for adults) force them to be more concerned about initial selection since future financing rests on a reasonable rate of success. Yet the PIC recognizes that to "cream off the top" is counterproductive if the aim of the JTPA is to help those who cannot find satisfactory employment on their own.

A related balancing act: extending the length of the training period would improve the odds that completers acquired the basic skills that employers were seeking. But the longer the training period, the fewer the number that can be accepted into training. Hence once again, the challenge to the PIC leadership is to find an optimal balance between length of training and the number accepted for training.

Even in the years of peak financing, the program was able to offer
services to no more than 10 to 20 percent of the eligible population.
In the face of this severe limitation, it is inevitable that all levels of the
political system—from the authorizing legislators to the implementing
bureaucrats—will strive to make the funds available to the largest number
of persons who could benefit from participation. This goes far to explain
why many staff members believed that the summer youth program was
too short both in its length and the hours of daily work; why many
PIC Referral Centers opted for sending clients out to jobs rather than
to training programs; and why the majority of training programs were
relatively short-term. These pressures on the JTPA administrators to
serve the optimal number of clients were built into the structure and
operation of the system.

A number of lessons for local administrators of JTPA programs can
be distilled from the Philadelphia PIC story. We will note and briefly
discuss some of the most important:

- The President and CEO of the Philadelphia PIC recognized that
  present and potential clients should be considered "customers" of
  the JTPA and that he and his staff had much to learn by periodically
  surveying these customers to discuss what was right and wrong
  about the ways in which the programs were being administered.
  The conventional perception that the program managers are the
  experts and what they do and do not do is right is a presumption,
  nothing more. In business service programs, the ways in which the
  clients perceive and respond to the program provide critical spurs
  to improved administration. Admittedly customer/client surveys are
  often difficult to design and expensive to implement, but the knowl-
  edge gained and the subsequent modifications can repay the costs
  many times over.
- Closely related to the foregoing is the need for simple, but admittedly
  difficult, follow-up information that extends beyond the required
  minimum thirty-day period. Since the principal aim of the JTPA is
  to assist marginally attached members of the labor force to make
  a transition into permanent, preferably private sector jobs, the
  prescribed follow-up period of 30 days is clearly inadequate. Exploratory efforts are needed, from postcard follow-ups to engaging
  the participation of selected employers to obtain information at a
  minimum of two, preferably three, follow-up points: three months,
  six months, and one year.
- The "Do Not Respond" (DNR) problem clearly invites more attention.
  The loss ratios all along the line—from the point of initial contact
  to a failure of a trainee to enter the labor market after completion

of a training program and the many opportunities for clients to drop out at different points along the way—require more attention. Clearly, people who have never worked or have not worked for a number of years are likely to be timid about contacting a service system that among other demands requires them to provide all sorts of documentary proof, including wage receipts and/or income tax returns. And it is not surprising that many, after initial or repeated contact, are overwhelmed and give up—at least temporarily. But the DNR problem is not solely a reflection of the weaknesses of the clients. The way the system operates—for instance by sending unprepared persons out to job openings—is indicative of the mal-functioning of the system, mistakes that can be reduced if not totally eliminated.

- The more informed the PIC becomes about the changing trends in the local labor market, the better its position to adjust its training programs, dropping some where the demand has slackened and expanding others where there are growing unmet needs.

Going beyond the confines of operational improvements, there are other areas where the PIC can do much, especially over the longer term, to help its clients. For instance:

- The placement record of the PIC depends in no small measure on the participation of the employer community. The larger the number of employers, especially those with above-minimum-wage entrance jobs, who look to the PIC as a reliable source for recruitment, the better its placement record and the better the reputation of the PIC among those who should seek out its services. Greater employer participation is especially important in the case of on-the-job training (OJT) positions for young minority adult males, many of whom will not fit into classroom training.
- In recent years, many states and some localities, as well as phi-lanthropy, have become important sources of funding for employment and training programs, adding to the revenues available to the PICs. This has been true for the Philadelphia PIC, and the better the job it does, the more access it is likely to have to further supplemental funding.
- Because of its diversified board membership and its growing rep-utation as a critically important Philadelphia service delivery agency, PIC is in a position to compete with other community agencies, to help broaden the opportunities for the hard-to-employ on a series of fronts where significant changes are called for but difficult to achieve. Specifically, it would be highly desirable if the municipal

government sought to make a limited number of opening jobs available to PIC trainees who have satisfactorily completed their training cycle. It would also represent a step forward if various trade unions that have more or less systematically excluded minorities could be persuaded to accept a limited number of qualified PIC completers if only to send a signal to the minority community that they are willing to adjust to the changing times. In this connection it is important to remember that almost 2 out of every 5 persons in Philadelphia are black. In addition, the PIC has a role to play—and it has begun to do so—in using its influence and leadership to explore the serious transportation situation that makes it next to impossible for inner-city persons to gain access to the expanding suburban job markets.

On the programmatic front, our study of the Philadelphia PIC leads us to suggest the following directions for program modifications in order to improve the transition of the hard-to-employ into regular jobs:

- Since we believe that it will be a long time until urban high schools in the nation's major cities are restructured so as to increase their holding power and improve their productivity in terms of the competences that its students and graduates command, we urge that the Philadelphia PIC pay increasing attention to the fourteen- and fifteen-year olds at risk of dropping out. The principal efforts should be to expand the summer youth program (with remedial educational services) into a year-round effort, to establish standards for admission and retention, and offer transitional assistance to high school graduates. We recognize that the PIC has begun to move in these directions and we recommend that it continue and expand its efforts along these lines.
- For the important group of young welfare mothers, clearly the help that they most need and want is in the area of child care. Except for a small number who can look to family members to assist them in such care, the vast majority require free or heavily subsidized care, particularly for preschool children between the ages of three and six; and afternoon care for children over six. Unless the state, the city, and the philanthropic community are able and willing to provide such heavily subsidized care, we believe that efforts to persuade welfare mothers to pursue training with an aim of getting jobs will prove ineffective.
- The most difficult challenge facing the Philadelphia PIC is to open more avenues for regular employment to young minority adult males, particularly between the ages of twenty-one and thirty-five, many

of whom have had only intermittent relations with the world of work. There is nothing easy about such an effort in the face of their limited competences and work records filled with long periods of unemployment. The likeliest ways for PIC to make progress with this group are to find some employers in the tightening labor market who would be willing to make some OJT and job slots available, to deliberately "cream" its applicant file to improve the probability of success, and, finally, to make some counseling staff available before, during, and after training, or until job assignment. There is no guarantee that these efforts will have a large payoff, but faced with the large number that are involved, such special efforts are called for. The best longer-term approach would be to reduce the number who drop out of high school and who keep swelling the pool as they age.

The foregoing suggests some of the directions for local action that could enhance PIC's contribution to the Philadelphia economy and society. The parallel challenge is to raise some issues and point some direction for national policy drawing not only on this material but on a half-century and more of the senior author's participation in the policy deliberations affecting employment and training policy.

One place to begin is to raise the question as to the goal of national employment and training policy, past, present, and future. One answer is to emphasize what the goal is not. The United States, unlike Sweden, has never been committed to a full employment economy, the Humphrey-Hawkins Act notwithstanding. The Swedes believe and have acted on the belief that every adult who is able and willing to work should be able to do so and they have been willing to invest up to 3 percent of their GNP to make this possible. By way of rough contrast, the United States currently invests about one-thirtieth of that amount. While we ostensibly continue to value the work ethic; while we have enjoyed a strong growth in total employment these past two decades; and while we are disconcerted by the large number of welfare families, we have basically shied away from making a national commitment to provide jobs for all who want to work. Although the Carter administration expanded public service employment to over 700,000, the program lost the support of the Democratic Congress in the late 1970s and the Reagan administration had little difficulty in eliminating it in the early 1980s.

Since full employment is clearly not a major national goal, at least not a goal to be achieved by large-scale federal actions, what is the logic underpinning the JTPA? An oversimplified answer is that the JTPA represents a continuing federal commitment to assist a limited number of hard-to-employ persons to obtain training and other services that will facilitate their transition into regular jobs. In structuring the program, the federal government looks to the lower levels of government to administer the program in partnership with the local business leadership. One of the aims of the program is to expand the supply of workers in areas where employers are actively hiring. Hence, one of the subsidiary goals of the JTPA is to improve the operations of local labor markets. But the first lesson from this summary appraisal is to underscore the question of scale and scope: how many people need help; how many are the JTPA able to help; what would be a reasonable national effort even if one stops short of a commitment to full employment? Clearly, one-hundredth of 1 percent of the GNP appears to be grossly inadequate in the face of unemployment levels in the 5 to 6 percent range and at the height of a five-year expansion. The only reasonable conclusion from the above is that the American people remain unpersuaded, even after more than a quarter century of experience, to make a large-scale continuing effort in employment and training programs. They are willing to keep doing a little, but they balk at doing a lot. Presumptively they believe that the labor market does not need all that much tinkering by the federal government and that most people who want to work will be able to find work on their own.

In 1988, after two decades of abortive reforms of the welfare system aimed at shifting the emphasis from income maintenance to assisting heads of households to become self-supporting, Congress is in the final stages of fashioning a bill that commanded large majorities in both houses and is likely to gain the President's approval. The thrust of the new legislation is clearly in favor of jobs over income maintenance, in favor of helping long-term welfare clients to move off the rolls into self-supporting jobs. Various states have been experimenting with workfare programs since the early 1980s, and while those which have addressed the problem seriously can show some gains, the evaluations suggest that large-scale movements of long-term welfare clients into regular jobs cannot be accomplished without substantial and sustained efforts, even in the face of a booming labor market.

Many of these clients need help to get jobs and many need income supplementation and other services (child care and Medicaid) if they are to maintain their families. While most people who go on welfare are able to get off within a two-year span, the new federal legislation and the earlier state experiments have been directed to the long-term cases, those on welfare for a decade or more. It would be hard to criticize the new orientation. All that one can point out is that in the absence of substantial up-front investment, long-term benefits are likely to remain problematic. It is far from clear that the necessary resources are adequately provided for in the new legislation, but if the public and the Congress are serious and remain serious about welfare reform, additional revenues must be forthcoming.

From a longer-term perspective, brief attention must be directed to some of the more important structural changes underway in the American society and economy that increase the need for stronger employment and training efforts at all levels and in all sectors—federal, state, and local—private and not-for-profit. About 3 out of every 4 Americans are employed in the service sector where literacy and numeracy as well as socialization competences (interactions with fellow workers and customers) are increasingly essential for getting and holding jobs. A disturbingly high percentage of youth, particularly metropolitan area minority youth, drop out of high school without such competences. In turn, a disturbingly high proportion of these young people, not only in their teens but in their twenties and later, are never able to establish effective linkages with the world of work. If the present rate of progress of urban educational reforms is indicative of future progress, it is clear that many of these young people will need access to "second-chance" opportunities. The Job Corps, the longest established of such second-chance opportunities, has a reasonable track record, but it is important to emphasize that it has been serving recently only between 40,000 to 50,000 applicants at approximately $15,000 each for a year-long enrollment. Second-chance opportunities do not come cheap.

In the growing national concern with drug trafficking, insufficient attention has been paid to its corrosive influence in weakening the stability of many inner-city neighborhoods and in providing the wrong signals for young people. Many adolescents come to view selling drugs as the quickest and best way for them to make money, which creates a powerful pull on them to drop out of school and to ignore the regular economy with its hard-to-obtain and low-paying entrance jobs. Aside from all of the other costs accruing from the growth of the illegal drug trade—from the increased number of homicides to the increased number of AIDs victims—the greatest threat of the off-the-record economy over time may turn out to be the derailment of many young people into a life of crime.

The last lesson that needs to be emphasized is that about two decades have passed since analysts first recognized the existence of a "Job Crisis for Black Youth." Despite this early recognition, progress has been appallingly slow which can best be explained by the disinclination of white Americans to recognize fully and respond effectively to the problems of blacks and Hispanics. But that places white Americans at serious risk since blacks and Hispanics account for between one-third and one-half of the total population of the nation's major urban centers. American democracy risks its future viability and surely its vitality if the citizenry continues to ignore the unresolved problems of its seriously deprived minorities. The greatest contribution of the JTPA in the end may turn out to be that it convinces Congress to improve and expand the program and thereby provide a structure for local businessmen, local government officials, and representatives of other local groups to cooperate in delivering constructive services to a population that must be assisted if it—and the nation at large—is to prosper.